Peace and Prosperity

1953 - 1961

Teachers Guide

A Supplemental Teaching Unit
from the Records of the National Archives

NATIONAL
ARCHIVES

National Archives Trust Fund Board
National Archives and Records Administration

A B C ⬙ C L I O

ABC – CLIO, Inc
130 Cremona Drive, P.O. Box 1911
Santa Barbara, CA 93116-1911
ISBN 1-57607-790-X

Other Units in this Series:

The Constitution: Evolution of a Government

The Bill of Rights: Evolution of Personal Liberties

The United States Expands West: 1785-1842

Westward Expansion: 1842-1912

The Civil War: Soldiers and Civilians

The Progressive Years: 1898-1917

World War I: The Home Front

The 1920's

The Great Depression and The New Deal

World War II: The Home Front

The United States At War: 1944

The Truman Years: 1945-1953

Table of Contents

*F*oreword

In its efforts to make the historical records of the federal government available nationally, the National Archives began a program in 1970 to introduce these vast resources to secondary school students. School classes visiting the National Archives in Washington were given the opportunity to examine and interpret original sources as historians use them. Teachers and students responded enthusiastically and encouraged the development of a series of supplemental teaching units.

Peace and Prosperity: 1953-1961 is the ninth unit in the series. It, like those that have preceded and will follow, is intended to bring you and your students the excitement and satisfaction of working with primary sources and to enhance your instructional program.

FRANK G. BURKE
Acting Archivist of the United States
1987

...to bring you and your students the excitement and satisfaction of working with primary sources and to enhance your instructional program.

Preface

◆ This unit is made up of 9 exercises.

◆ Each exercise includes reproductions of documents from the National Archives and suggests classroom activities based on these documents.

Peace and Prosperity: 1953-1961 is a teaching unit designed to supplement your students' study of the 1950s. The unit is made up of nine exercises. Each exercise includes reproductions of documents from the National Archives and suggests classroom activities based on these documents. The documents include official correspondence, telegrams, photographs, political cartoons, pamphlets, maps, and court decisions. Students practice the historian's skills as they complete exercises, using these documents to gather information, identify points of view, evaluate evidence, form hypotheses, and draw conclusions.

The documents in this unit do not reflect every topic usually included in a history textbook. In some instances the federal government had no interest or authority over a given event and therefore compiled no records on it. In other cases documents in the National Archives on several historic topics proved to be difficult to use in the classroom due to the recent nature of the documents. Many textbooks treat the postwar period as a whole, so teachers may find it useful to use the companion unit, *The Truman Years: 1945-1953*, along with this one.

Peace and Prosperity: 1953-1961 is useful in the government classroom as well as the history classroom. Activities included in exercises 3, 5, 6, and 7 are designed specifically for use by government and civics teachers.

National Archives education specialists Wynell Burroughs Schamel, Jean M. West and Leslie Gray and education branch chief Elsie Freeman Finch developed this publication. We are pleased to issue a revised and updated set of these documentary teaching materials.

WYNELL B. SCHAMEL
LEE ANN POTTER
Education Specialists
2001

Peace and Prosperity: 1953-1961 is a teaching unit designed to supplement your students' study of the 1950s. It is useful in the government classroom as well as the history classroom.

Acknowledgments

Many people helped in the original production of this unit. They include National Archives staff members Pat El-Ashry, Paul Conner, Joseph Fernandez, Cindy Fox, Jennie Guildbaud, Nancy McGovern, Tom Nastick, Dian Palmer, Jimmy Rush, Kathy Struss, Fred Walters, Karl Weissenbach, John Vernon, and Alison Wilson.

Arthur Pease, a classroom teacher in Lebanon, NH, and other social studies teachers reviewed elements of this unit. Their reactions and comments have shaped and improved the document selection and the teaching exercises.

Frank G. Burke, Acting Archivist of the United States; Edith James, Director of the Exhibits and Educational Programs Division; David Kepley, Chief of the Legislative Reference Branch; Kathy Struss, archivist, Dwight D. Eisenhower Presidential Library; and John E. Wickman, Director of the Dwight D. Eisenhower Presidential Library, reviewed the unit for historical content. [Positions held at time of original publication.]

During the republication process, we were ably assisted by George Mason University intern Adam Jevec; volunteers Donald Alderson, Elizabeth S. Lourie, and Jane Douma Pearson; and National Archives staff members Michael Hussey, A.J. Daverede, Patrick Osborn, Amy Patterson, Kate Flaherty, Donald Roe, and Charles Mayn.

Publisher's Note

Primary source documents have long been a cornerstone of ABC-CLIO's commitment to producing high-quality, learner-centered history and social studies resources. When our nation's students have the opportunity to interact with the undiluted artifacts of the past, they can better understand the breadth of the human experience and the present state of affairs.

It is with great enthusiasm that we celebrate the release of this series of teaching units designed in partnership with the National Archives—materials that we hope will bring historical context and deeper knowledge to U.S. middle and high school students. Each unit has been revised and updated, including new bibliographic references. Each teaching unit has been correlated to the curriculum standards for the teaching of social studies and history developed by the National Council for the Social Studies and the National Center for History in the Schools.

For more effective use of these teaching units in the classroom, each booklet is accompanied by an interactive CD-ROM which includes exercise worksheets, digital images of original documents, and, for four titles, sound recordings. A videocassette of motion pictures accompanies the teaching unit *The United States At War: 1944*. For those who would like to order facsimiles of primary source documents in their original sizes, or additional titles in this series, we have included an order form to make it easy for you to do so.

The mission of the National Archives is "to ensure ready access to the essential evidence that documents the rights of American citizens, the actions of Federal officials, and the national experience."

These units go a long way toward fulfilling that mission, helping the next generation of American citizens develop a clear understanding of the nation's past and a firm grasp of the role of the individual in guiding the nation's future. ABC-CLIO is honored to be part of this process.

BECKY SNYDER
Publisher & Vice President
ABC-CLIO Schools

> The mission of the National Archives is "to ensure ready access to the essential evidence that documents the rights of American citizens, the actions of Federal officials, and the national experience."

Teaching With Documents Curriculum Standards Correlations

The National Council for the Social Studies and the National Center for History in the Schools have developed a set of comprehensive curriculum standards for the teaching of social studies and history. Take a look at how thoroughly the Teaching With Documents series supports the curriculum.

National Council for the Social Studies

Standard	Peace and Prosperity: 1953–1961	The Truman Years: 1945–1953	The United States At War: 1944	War II: The Home Front	The Great Depression and The New Deal World	The 1920's	World War I: The Home Front	The Progressive Years: 1898–1917	The Civil War: Soldiers and Civilians	Westward Expansion: 1842–1912	The United States Expands West: 1785–1842	The Bill of Rights: Evolution of Personal Liberties	The Constitution: Evolution of a Government
CULTURE—should provide for the study of culture and cultural diversity	•			•		•				•	•		•
TIME, CONTINUITY & CHANGE—should provide for the study of the ways people view themselves in and over time			•	•							•	•	•
PEOPLE, PLACES & ENVIRONMENT—should provide for the study of people, places, and environments					•	•	•	•	•	•	•	•	•
INDIVIDUAL DEVELOPMENT & IDENTITY—should provide for the study of individual development and identity	•				•	•	•	•	•	•	•	•	•
INDIVIDUALS, GROUPS & INSTITUTIONS—should provide for the study of interactions among individuals, groups, and institutions	•	•	•		•	•		•	•	•	•	•	•
POWER, AUTHORITY & GOVERNANCE—should provide for the study of how structures of power are created and changed	•	•			•	•		•		•	•	•	•
PRODUCTION, DISTRIBUTION & CONSUMPTION—should provide for the study of the usage of goods and services		•			•	•		•		•	•		•
SCIENCE, TECHNOLOGY & SOCIETY—should provide for the study of relationships among science, technology, and society		•	•			•		•	•	•			
GLOBAL CONNECTIONS—should provide for the study of global connections and interdependence	•	•	•					•			•		•
CIVIC IDEALS & PRACTICES—should provide for the study of the ideals, principles, and practices of citizenship			•			•						•	•

National Center for History in the Schools

Standard	Peace and Prosperity: 1953–1961	The Truman Years: 1945–1953	The United States At War: 1944	War II: The Home Front	The Great Depression and The New Deal World	The 1920's	World War I: The Home Front	The Progressive Years: 1898–1917	The Civil War: Soldiers and Civilians	Westward Expansion: 1842–1912	The United States Expands West: 1785–1842	The Bill of Rights: Evolution of Personal Liberties	The Constitution: Evolution of a Government
CHRONOLOGICAL THINKING	•	•	•	•	•	•	•	•	•	•	•	•	•
HISTORICAL COMPREHENSION	•	•	•	•	•	•	•	•	•	•	•	•	•
HISTORICAL ANALYSIS & INTERPRETATION	•	•	•	•	•	•	•	•	•	•	•	•	•
HISTORICAL RESEARCH CAPABILITIES	•	•	•	•	•	•	•	•	•	•	•	•	
HISTORICAL ISSUES-ANALYSIS & DECISION-MAKING	•	•	•	•	•	•	•	•	•	•	•	•	•

Introduction

This unit contains two elements: 1) a book, which contains a teachers guide and a set of reproductions of print documents, and 2) a CD-ROM, which contains the exercise worksheets from the teachers guide, a set of reproductions of print documents, and sound recordings in electronic format. In selecting the documents, we applied three standards. First, the documents must be entirely from the holdings of the National Archives and must reflect the actions of the federal government or citizens' responses to those actions. Second, each document must be typical of the hundreds of records of its kind relating to its particular topic. Third, the documents must be legible or audible and potentially useful for vocabulary development. In selecting documents we attempted to choose those having appeal to young people.

UNIT CONTAINS:

◆ **1)** a book, which contains a teachers guide and a set of reproductions of print documents, and

◆ **2)** a CD-ROM, which contains the exercise worksheets from the teachers guide and a set of reproductions of print documents and sound recordings in electronic format.

Objectives

We have provided an outline of the general objectives for the unit. You will be able to achieve these objectives by completing several, if not all, of the exercises in the unit. Because each exercise aims to develop skills defined in the general objectives, you may be selective and still develop those skills. In addition, each exercise has its own specific objectives.

Outline

This unit on the 1950s includes 9 exercises, 8 of which relate to social, political, and military issues of the decade. Exercise 9 is a summary exercise focused on possible careers and life-long interest in history.

List of Documents

The list of documents gives specific information (e.g., date and name of author) and record group number for each document. Records in the National Archives are arranged in record groups. A typical record group (RG) consists of the records created or accumulated by a department, agency, bureau, or other administrative unit of the federal government. Each record group is identified for retrieval purposes by a record group number; for example, RG 51 (Office of Management and Budget) or RG 218 (U.S. Joint Chiefs of Staff). Complete archival citations of all documents are listed in the appendix, p. 60.

Exercise Summary Chart

The chart shows the organization of the nine exercises. For each exercise the chart outlines the materials needed, the document content, the student activities that are emphasized, and the number of class periods needed. Review the chart carefully and decide which exercises to use based on your objectives for the students, their ability levels, and the content you wish to teach. The exercises may be adapted to fit your objectives and teaching style.

Introductory Exercises

Before starting exercises 1-9, it is important to familiarize students with documents and their importance to the historian who interprets them and writes history from them. We suggest that you direct students to do one or all of the introductory exercises. The Historian's Tools, p. 11, is designed to increase students' awareness of the process of analyzing historical information and is most appropriate for students working at or above ninth grade reading level. The Written Document Analysis, p. 13, is designed to help students analyze systematically any written document in this unit. The Photograph Analysis, p. 14, can be used for the same purpose with any of the photographs in the unit. The Sound Recording Analysis, p. 15, can be used to help students listen to sound recordings to retrieve historical information. The Cartoon Analysis, p. 17, can be used to analyze systematically political cartoons.

Classroom Exercises

This unit contains nine suggested exercises. Within the explanatory material for each of the exercises, you will find the following information:

➤ Note to the teacher   ➤ Materials needed

➤ Classroom time required   ➤ Procedures

➤ Objectives (specific)   ➤ Student worksheets

You may choose to combine several exercises on a topic within the unit. In some instances a document is used in more than one exercise when appropriate to the skill or content objectives. We encourage you to select and adapt the exercises and documents that best suit your own teaching style.

Ability Levels

As in our other units, we have developed exercises for students of different abilities. For some topics, we have designed two or more procedures, tailored to different student needs. Throughout the unit we have made an effort to provide exercises in which students utilize a variety of skills, including reading for understanding, interpreting maps and cartoons, and analyzing legislation and court cases. All lessons have procedures for ability levels one, two, and three. Procedures begin with strategies designed for level three students, continue with level two strategies, and conclude with level one strategies. Our definition of each ability level is as follows:

Level One: Good reading skills, ability to organize and interpret information from several sources with minimal direction from teacher, and ability to complete assignments independently.

Level Two: Average reading skills, ability to organize and interpret information from several sources with general direction from teacher, and ability to complete assignments with some assistance from teacher.

Level Three: Limited reading skills, and ability to organize and interpret information from several sources with step-by-step direction from teacher, and ability to complete assignments with close supervision from teacher.

These ability levels are merely guides. We recognize that you will adapt the exercises to suit your students' needs and your own teaching style.

Time Line

A time line is included for use by your students. You may want to reproduce it for each student or display it.

Bibliography

As students work with the documents, they should be assigned appropriate readings from their text and other secondary sources. They should also be encouraged to use the resources of school and public libraries. To guide them, an annotated bibliography appears at the end of the Teachers Guide.

General Objectives

Upon successfully completing the exercises in this unit, students should be able to demonstrate the following skills using a single document:

➤ Identify factual evidence

➤ Identify points of view (bias and/or prejudice)

➤ Collect, reorder, and weigh the significance of evidence

➤ Develop defensible inferences, conclusions, and generalizations from factual information

Using several documents from this unit, students should be able to:

➤ Analyze the documents to compare and contrast evidence

➤ Evaluate and interpret evidence drawn from the documents

Fight
Communism

with

"Truth Dollars"
for Radio Free Europe

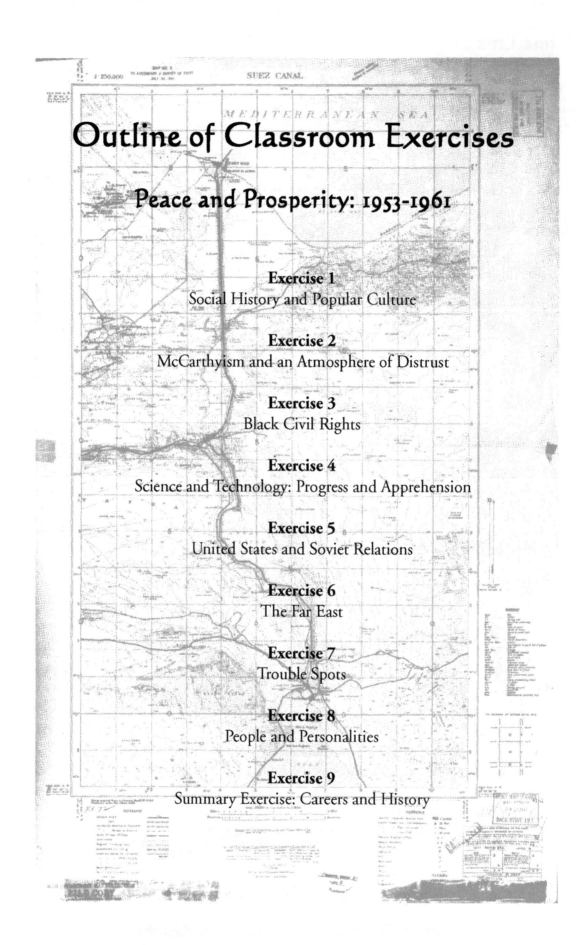

Outline of Classroom Exercises

Peace and Prosperity: 1953-1961

Exercise 1
Social History and Popular Culture

Exercise 2
McCarthyism and an Atmosphere of Distrust

Exercise 3
Black Civil Rights

Exercise 4
Science and Technology: Progress and Apprehension

Exercise 5
United States and Soviet Relations

Exercise 6
The Far East

Exercise 7
Trouble Spots

Exercise 8
People and Personalities

Exercise 9
Summary Exercise: Careers and History

List of Documents

Following the identifying information for each document reproduced in the unit, we have given the record group (RG) number in which the original can be found. Should you want copies of these documents or, for other reasons, wish to refer to them in correspondence with us, give the complete archival citation, which is found in the appendix on page 59. **You may duplicate any of the documents in this unit for use with your students.**

Documents in *Peace and Prosperity: 1953-1961* are taken from the following record groups: Office of Management and Budget (RG 51), Office of the Chief of Engineers (RG 77), National Archives Collection of Donated Materials (RG 200), U.S. Joint Chiefs of Staff (RG 218), U.S. House of Representatives (RG 233), Supreme Court of the United States (RG 267), U.S. Information Agency (RG 306), and Headquarters of the U.S. Air Force (RG 341). Additional documents are taken from the holdings of the Dwight D. Eisenhower Presidential Library.

1. Photograph of President Eisenhower and Mamie Eisenhower watching Richard Nixon's "Checkers speech" on television, September 23, 1952 (Dwight D. Eisenhower Presidential Library). © by Wide World Photos, Inc. Used with permission.

2. Photograph of President Eisenhower, Roy Rogers, Dale Evans, and others attending grandson David Eisenhower's birthday party, March 31, 1956 (Dwight D. Eisenhower Presidential Library).

3. Photograph of President Eisenhower with Jane Powell, Bob Hope, Pearl Bailey, and others, June 7, 1956 (Dwight D. Eisenhower Presidential Library).

4. Photograph of President Eisenhower throwing out the ball for the opening game of the 1956 World Series, October 3, 1956 (Dwight D. Eisenhower Presidential Library). © by I.H.T. Corporation. Used with permission.

5. The Advertising Council brochure entitled "The Future of America," 1954 (Dwight D. Eisenhower Presidential Library).

6. Photograph of Senator Joseph R. McCarthy, March 14, 1950 (RG 306).

7. Enabling decision in *Brown v. Board of Education of Topeka, Kansas*, May 31, 1955 (RG 267).

8. Text of Presidential address released to the press regarding the Little Rock crisis, September 24, 1957 (Dwight D. Eisenhower Presidential Library).

9. House Resolution 6127, April 1, 1957 (RG 233).

10. House Report No. 291, April 1, 1957 (RG 233).

11. Morrow's memo to Eisenhower regarding the student protest movement in the South, March 7, 1960 (Dwight D. Eisenhower Presidential Library).

12. Postal workers union resolution calling upon President Eisenhower to conduct a civil rights fact-finding tour of the South, April 6, 1957 (Dwight D. Eisenhower Presidential Library).

13. Photograph of President Eisenhower with Dr. Jonas Salk, inventor of the polio vaccine, April 22, 1955 (Dwight D. Eisenhower Presidential Library). © by Wide World Photos, Inc. Used with permission.

14. Cadle's memo to the director of the Military Division regarding the space race, March 2, 1960 (RG 51).

15. Civil Defense poster "How Could You Know Tonight was the Night?" 1954 (Dwight D. Eisenhower Presidential Library).

16. U.S. Air Force report of a UFO sighting, December 3, 1957 (RG 341).

17. Photograph of President Eisenhower with young pianist Van Cliburn, May 23, 1958 (Dwight D. Eisenhower Presidential Library).

18. Translation of Khrushchev's letter to Eisenhower upon the visit of Vice President Nixon to the Soviet Union, August 1959 (Dwight D. Eisenhower Presidential Library).

19. White House memo regarding U.S. objectives in Khrushchev's visit, September 11, 1959 (Dwight D. Eisenhower Presidential Library).

20. Photograph of Moscow exhibit of the downed U-2 plane, May 1960 (Dwight D. Eisenhower Presidential Library).

21. Special staff note on the breakup of the Paris summit, May 19, 1960 (Dwight D. Eisenhower Presidential Library).

22. Revised draft of statement by President Eisenhower regarding the Korean armistice, July 26, 1953 (Dwight D. Eisenhower Presidential Library).

23. Cummings' letter to Eisenhower about her son, Barnard Cummings, a prisoner of war, September 6, 1953 (Dwight D. Eisenhower Presidential Library).

24. Mutual Defense Treaty between the United States and Korea, October 1, 1953 (RG 218).

25. Memo, "A Concept for Action with Regard to Indochina," May 13, 1954 (RG 218).

26. Diem's letter to Eisenhower on the fifth anniversary of the Republic of Vietnam, November 8, 1960 (Dwight D. Eisenhower Presidential Library).

27. Memo from Lederer to Stump, reporting on refugees, August 30, 1954 (RG 218).

28. Memo from Smith to Gray regarding the internal political situation in Iran, September 5, 1958 (Dwight D. Eisenhower Presidential Library).

29. Translation of telegram from Guatemalan President Fuentes to Eisenhower, November 19, 1960 (Dwight D. Eisenhower Presidential Library).

30. Advertisement for Radio Free Europe, 1954 (Dwight D. Eisenhower Presidential Library).

31. Photograph of Hungarian freedom fighters riding on a captured Soviet T-55 tank, October 1956 (RG 306). © by Wide World Photos. Used with permission.

32. Map of Suez Canal, July 30, 1941 (RG 77).

33. Cartoon, "Images of the Fifties," January 1961 (Dwight D. Eisenhower Presidential Library © by *Deseret News*. Used with permission.

34. *Washington Post* article, The Gallup Poll, August 7, 1955 (Dwight D. Eisenhower Presidential Library). © by The Gallup Poll. Used with permission.

35. Photograph of President Eisenhower and congressional leaders, March 6, 1959 (Dwight D. Eisenhower Presidential Library).

36. Photograph of Senator Margaret Chase Smith, n.d. (RG 306).

37. Photograph of President Eisenhower with Billy Graham, August 8, 1952 (Dwight D. Eisenhower Presidential Library).

38. Fans' letter to Eisenhower regarding the induction of Elvis Presley into the Army, March 1958 (Dwight D. Eisenhower Presidential Library).

39. Translation of letter from French President de Gaulle to Eisenhower, May 20, 1960 (Dwight D. Eisenhower Presidential Library).

40. Photograph of Khrushchev and Eisenhower at Camp David, September 25, 1959 (Dwight D. Eisenhower Presidential Library).

Sound Recordings on CD-ROM

Sound recording A. Army-McCarthy hearings with Joseph McCarthy, Roy Cohn, and Joseph Welch, June 9, 1954 (National Archives Collection of Donated Materials). © by CBS Inc. Used with permission.

Sound recording B. Rev. Dr. Martin Luther King, Jr., on "Meet the Press," 1960 (National Archives Collection of Donated Materials). © by CBS Inc. Used with permission.

Sound recording C. Yucca Flats Atomic Tests reported by Charles Collingwood, March 17, 1953 (National Archives Collection of Donated Materials). © by CBS Inc. Used with permission.

Sound recording D. "Kitchen debate" between Nikita Khrushchev and Nixon, July 24, 1959 (National Archives Collection of Donated Materials).

Sound recording E. Farewell address by Dwight D. Eisenhower, January 17, 1960 (National Archives Collection of Donated Materials).

Exercise Summary Chart

EXERCISE	NUMBER OF DOCUMENTS	CONTENT	STUDENT ACTIVITIES	NUMBER OF CLASS PERIODS
1. Social History and Popular Culture Documents 1-5 Worksheet 1 Photograph Analysis worksheet	5	Postwar changes in American life	Analyzing photographs Working in groups Creative writing	1-3
2. McCarthyism and an Atmosphere of Distrust Documents 6 and 30 Sound Recording A Sound Recording Analysis worksheet	2	The postwar Communist scare	Interpreting a sound recording Identifying cause and effect Analyzing documents and coming to conclusions	1-2
3. Black Civil Rights Documents 7-12 and 35 Sound Recording B Worksheet 2 Written Document Analysis worksheet	7	Postwar civil rights movement programs	Establishing a chronology of events Reading for main ideas Role-playing	1-3
4. Science and Technology: Progress and Apprehension Documents 13-16 Sound Recording C Worksheet 3	4	Changes in American life brought about by science and technology	Interpreting a photograph Decision-making Role-playing	1-2
5. United States and Soviet Relations Documents 17-21 Sound Recording D worksheet 4	5	Soviet-American relations during the Eisenhower administration	Developing vocabulary Analyzing documents and coming to a conclusion Writing a position paper	1-2
6. The Far East Documents 22-27 Worksheet 5	6	U.S. policy in Korea and Vietnam during the 1950s	Analyzing documents and coming to conclusions Comparing and contrasting American policy between Korea and Vietnam	1-2
7. Trouble Spots Documents 28-22 Worksheet 6	5	U.S. policy in response to nationalism and communism	Interpreting a map Researching related topics	1-2

EXERCISE	NUMBER OF DOCUMENTS	CONTENT	STUDENT ACTIVITIES	NUMBER OF CLASS PERIODS
8. People and Personalities Documents 33-40 Sound Recordings B and E	8	Prominent figures of the 1950s	Interpreting a sound recording Developing a plan based on research Evaluating the historical accuracy of a fictional account of an event	1-3
9. Summary Exercise: Careers and History Documents 1-40 Sound Recordings A-E	40	Applications of history	Designing and preparing projects that demonstrate an application of the history and content of a group of documents	1 term

Introductory Exercises

These exercises introduce students to the general objectives of the unit. They focus students' attention on documents and their importance to the historian, who interprets and records the past. They serve as valuable opening exercises for this unit.

The Historian's Tools

The Historian's Tools worksheet is designed to increase students' awareness of the process of analyzing historical information. It focuses on both the nature of the process of analyzing historical information and those factors that influence the historian's analysis of evidence. The worksheet includes specific questions on distinctions between primary and secondary sources, the reliability of those sources, and the influence of bias, point of view, and perspective on the historian's interpretation.

Students do not analyze documents to complete this worksheet as they do in other exercises in the unit. Class discussion, however, is essential to helping students understand the issues raised by the worksheet because there are many ways to answer the questions. You may wish to assign the worksheet as homework and discuss it with students in class.

Written Document Analysis

The Written Document Analysis worksheet helps students to analyze systematically any written document in this unit. In sections 1-5 of the worksheet, students locate basic details within the document. In section 6 students analyze the document more critically as they complete items A-E. There are many possible correct answers to section 6, A-E. We suggest you use either document 6, 9, 10, or 38 with this worksheet.

Photograph Analysis

The Photograph Analysis worksheet helps students to identify systematically the historical evidence within photographs. It is designed to improve students' ability to use photographs as historical documents. It can be used specifically with exercises 1, 2, 4, 7, and 8.

Sound Recording Analysis

The Sound Recording Analysis worksheet helps students to identify systematically the historical evidence within recordings. It is designed to improve students' ability to listen to sound recordings as primary sources of historical information. It can be used specifically with exercises 2, 3, 4, 5, and 8.

Cartoon Analysis

The Cartoon Analysis worksheet helps students to analyze systematically any cartoon in this unit. It is designed to improve students' ability to analyze the visual and written information contained in political cartoons. It can be used specifically with exercise 8.

HOW COULD YOU KNOW
TONIGHT WAS THE NIGHT?

Everything was peaceful when you went to bed.

Not a hint of war on the late newscast.

How could you know they'd choose our town, tonight?

You couldn't. The enemy didn't want you to know.

*   *   *

But you could have been ready. Atomic bombs—and tornadoes, fires, floods—strike without warning. It's so important to be ready. So easy, too, now that U. S. Civil Defense has prepared a list of "must" first-aid items. Any drug counter can supply them. Every home should have them. Every family should learn how to use them.

BE SURE YOU HAVE THESE OFFICIAL DISASTER FIRST-AID ITEMS IN YOUR HOME

- ☐ 4 Triangular Bandages
- ☐ 12 Sterile Gauze Pads (3" x 3")
- ☐ 1 Gauze Bandage (2" x 10 yds.)
- ☐ 1 Gauze Bandage (1" x 10 yds.)
- ☐ 2 Large Emergency Dressings (7½" x 8")
- ☐ 100 Water-Purification Tablets (4 mg.)

- ☐ 3 oz. Antiseptic, Benzalkonium Chloride
- ☐ 1 oz. Aromatic Spirits of Ammonia
- ☐ 1 oz. Castor Oil Eye Drops
- ☐ 50 Sodium Chloride Tablets (10 gr.)
- ☐ 50 Sodium Bicarbonate Tablets (5 gr.)
- ☐ 12 Wooden Tongue Blades

Get free booklet "Emergency Action To Save Lives" from your drug counter or local Civil Defense Director.

 ———————————————

SPONSOR'S NAME

CD-106   3 cols. x 166 lines (498 lines)

The Historian's Tools

Worksheet

1. If you were writing a chapter in your textbook on the 1950s, list three things you would like to know about that period.

    1. _____
    2. _____
    3. _____

2. Where might you look to find information about the three topics you listed in #1?

Topic	Source of Information
_____	_____
_____	_____
_____	_____

3. Historians classify sources of information as **PRIMARY** or **SECONDARY**. Primary sources are those created by people who actually saw or participated in an event and recorded that event or their reactions to it immediately after the event. Secondary sources are those created by someone either not present when that event occurred or removed from it by time. Classify the sources of information you listed in #2 as either primary or secondary by placing a **P** or **S** next to your answers in #2. Reconsider the sources you would use to find information about the postwar period; list three more here:

    1. _____
    2. _____
    3. _____

4. Some sources of historical information are viewed as more **RELIABLE** than others, though all of them may be useful. Factors such as bias, self-interest, distance, and faulty memory affect the reliability of a source. Below is a list of sources of information on the nuclear test at Yucca Flats, March 17, 1953. Rate the reliability of each source on a numerical scale in which 1 is reliable and 5 very unreliable. Be able to support your ratings.

    A. A Department of Defense plan for deployment
    of troops during the nuclear test.   1   2   3   4   5

    B. A recording by a reporter at the nuclear test site.   1   2   3   4   5

    C. A newspaper article written the day after
    the nuclear test.   1   2   3   4   5

D. A transcript of an interview conducted
    with an eyewitness 8 years after the nuclear test.   1   2   3   4   5

E. A U.S. history high school textbook description
    of the development of nuclear weapons.   1   2   3   4   5

F. A description of the development of
    nuclear weapons in an encyclopedia.   1   2   3   4   5

5. What personal and social factors might influence historians as they write about people and
    events of the past?

    _____

    _____

    _____

6. What personal and social factors influence *you* as you read historical accounts of people
    and events?

    _____

    _____

    _____

Designed and developed by the education staff of the National Archives and Records Administration, Washington, DC 20408.

Written Document Analysis

Worksheet

1. Type of Document (Check one):
   - _____ Newspaper
   - _____ Letter
   - _____ Patent
   - _____ Memorandum
   - _____ Map
   - _____ Telegram
   - _____ Press release
   - _____ Report
   - _____ Advertisement
   - _____ Congressional record
   - _____ Census report
   - _____ Other

2. Unique Physical Qualities of the Document (check one or more):
   - _____ Interesting letterhead
   - _____ Handwritten
   - _____ Typed
   - _____ Seals
   - _____ Notations
   - _____ "RECEIVED" stamp
   - _____ Other

3. Date(s) of Document: _____

4. Author (or creator) of the Document: _____

   Position (Title): _____

5. For What Audience was the Document Written? _____

6. Document Information (There are many possible ways to answer A-E.)

   A. List three things the author said that you think are important:

      1. _____
      2. _____
      3. _____

   B. Why do you think this document was written?

      _____

      _____

   C. What evidence in the document helps you to know why it was written?
      Quote from the document.

      _____

      _____

   D. List two things the document tells you about life in the United States
      at the time it was written:

      1. _____
      2. _____

   E. Write a question to the author that is left unanswered by the document:

      _____

      _____

Designed and developed by the education staff of the National Archives and Records Administration, Washington, DC 20408.

Photograph Analysis

Worksheet

Step 1. Observation

A. Study the photograph for 2 minutes. Form an overall impression of the photograph and then examine individual items. Next, divide the photo into quadrants and study each section to see what new details become visible.

B. Use the chart below to list people, objects, and activities in the photograph.

PEOPLE	OBJECTS	ACTIVITIES
_____	_____	_____
_____	_____	_____
_____	_____	_____
_____	_____	_____
_____	_____	_____
_____	_____	_____

Step 2. Inference

Based on what you have observed above, list three things you might infer from this photograph:

1. _____
2. _____
3. _____

Step 3. Questions

A. What questions does this photograph raise in your mind?

_____
_____

B. Where could you find answers to them?

_____
_____

Designed and developed by the education staff of the National Archives and Records Administration, Washington, DC 20408.

Sound Recording Analysis

Worksheet

Step 1. Pre-listening

A. Whose voices will you hear on this recording? _____

_____

B. What is the date of this recording? _____

C. Where was this recording made? _____

Step 2. Listening

A. Type of sound recording (check one):

_____ Policy speech	_____ Congressional testimony
_____ News report	_____ Interview
_____ Entertainment broadcast	_____ Press conference
_____ Convention proceedings	_____ Campaign speech
_____ Arguments before a court	_____ Other
_____ Panel discussion	

B. Unique physical qualities of the recording

_____ Music	_____ Special sound effects
_____ Live broadcast	_____ Background sound
_____ Narrated	

C. What is the tone or mood of this sound recording? _____

_____

Step 3. Post-listening (or repeated listening)

A. List three things in this sound recording that you think are important:

1. _____

2. _____

3. _____

B. Why do you think the original broadcast was made and for what audience?

_____

_____

C. What evidence in the recording helps you to know why it was made?

_____

_____

D. List two things this sound recording tells you about life in the United States at the time it was made:

1. _____

2. _____

E. Write a question to the broadcaster that is left unanswered by this sound recording:

_____

_____

F. What information do you gain about this event that would not be conveyed by a written transcript? Be specific.

_____

_____

Designed and developed by the education staff of the National Archives and Records Administration, Washington, DC 20408.

Cartoon Analysis

Worksheet

Visuals	Words (not all cartoons include words)
Step One 1. List the objects or people you see in the cartoon.	1. Identify the cartoon caption and/ or title. 2. Locate three words or phrases used by the cartoonist to identify objects or people within the cartoon. 3. Record any important dates or numbers that appear in the cartoon.
Step Two 2. Which of the objects on your list are symbols? 3. What do you think each symbol means?	4. Which words or phrases in the cartoon appear to be the most significant? Why do you think so? 5. List adjectives that describe the emotions portrayed in the cartoon.

Step Three

A. Describe the action taking place in the cartoon.

B. Explain how the words in the cartoon clarify the symbols.

C. Explain the message of the cartoon.

D. What special interest groups would agree/disagree with the cartoon's message? Why?

Designed and developed by the education staff of the National Archives and Records Administration, Washington, DC 20408.

Exercise 1
Social History and Popular Culture

Note to the Teacher:

Having moved into the public consciousness only in the late 1940s, television so captured the 1950s that by that decade's end at least four out of five homes had television sets. In **document 1** President and Mrs. Eisenhower gaze upon an early television set. The visual appeal and immediacy of telecasts ensured that viewers would tune into all manner of programming — whatever its quality — and react to the accompanying commercial advertisements. Television has proved a superb medium for promoting a variety of "necessary" products before a vast audience.

For example, Roy Rogers' status as the "King of the Cowboys," established in Western movies of the forties, was considerably enhanced in the fifties as numerous children watched him weekly on his own television show and urged their mothers to buy products promoted by that program. The influence of Roy and his wife Dale Evans (the "Queen of the Cowgirls," naturally) are reflected in **document 2** as they helped Ike's grandson, David, celebrate his birthday.

But it was not just cowboy stars who profited from television's versatility. Many radio, stage, and screen actors gained new or added exposure as did politicians, newscasters, comedians, and sports figures. In **document 3**, prominent 1950s entertainers, including Jane Powell, Bob Hope, and Pearl Bailey, joined President Eisenhower to attend the 1956 White House News Photographers Association Dinner.

To professional baseball and football promoters, television's ability to bring games to large home audiences soon began to transcend other, more conventional, measures of success. Game times were arranged to suit commercial sponsors, and players' salaries increased wildly as the more glamorous performers became media darlings, particularly in large cities where they could also give sophisticated interviews. Owners of teams began to regard a season as successful more on the basis of television revenues than upon the number of fans actually attending the games. In actuality, both attendance and telecast income began to rise substantially.

Document 4 shows the President throwing out the first ball for the opening game of the 1956 World Series between the New York Yankees and the Brooklyn Dodgers, the top teams in the American League and National League, respectively. This series was the last of the "subway series," in which fans could attend all games by merely taking the subway between team parks. After the 1957 season, the owners moved two teams westward, the Dodgers to Los Angeles and the New York Giants to San Francisco, in search of California gold.

The 1956 series also showcased a "perfect game" pitched by Yankee journeyman Don Larsen. This was the only time anyone ever pitched a no-hitter in postseason play. In addition, the later Baseball Hall of Famers — Mickey Mantle, Whitey Ford, and Yogi Berra for the Yankees; Jackie Robinson, Roy Campanella, and Duke Snider for the Dodgers — played prominent roles.

Television both contributed to and benefited from the mass consumerism sweeping the postwar United States in the 1950s. Introduced to credit cards, a robust economy, and advertising that depicted spending as truly patriotic and necessary, an expanding middle class bought and bought big. What Americans thought they needed most beyond a strong national defense were convenience items, such as electric blenders, refrigerators, mixers, garbage disposals, and dishwashers, not to mention big-finned cars, camper trailers, sports boats, "TV dinners," and, of course, television sets. America's optimism in the 1950s about its capacity to shape society's future is captured in **document 5**.

As a result of rapid population growth and its consequent effect on already congested city housing and services, urban dwellers sought escape in the outlying suburbs. A federally funded 41,000-mile highway system began to make travel to and from work easier and to provide impetus for vacations all across the country. For those yearning to visit exotic places, there were the new jet planes to take them anywhere swiftly and safely.

The workplace was being transformed as well. Continuing the wartime trend, more and more women were entering the job market. Computers and other work-saving devices, such as dictaphones and electric typewriters, were gradually being introduced; the Atomic Energy Commission had 3 IBM 701 computers.

The 1950s were characterized by tremendous change and growth. It was a decade in which many phenomena that we now take for granted first became culturally significant. The decade was a key transitional time to the present.

Time: 1 to 3 class periods

Objectives:

- To describe changes in American life following World War II.

- To project the future impact of a demographic group.

Materials Needed:

Documents 1-5, 35-39
Photograph Analysis worksheet, p. 14
Worksheet 1

Procedures:

1. Divide the class into groups of 5 students each. Duplicate copies of documents 1-5 for each group and a Photograph Analysis worksheet for each student. Direct each student to analyze one document. Distribute worksheet 1 to each student and direct students to circulate document 5 to complete the worksheet. Once the worksheets are complete, review each document with the class.

2. Ask students to collect information on U.S. popular culture in the postwar years from documents 35-39, their textbooks, adults who recall the time period, and other primary and secondary sources. It would be helpful to suggest sample interview questions for your students. Assign a journal writing exercise giving the following directions: Imagine you are a middle class U.S. teenager, born in 1946, living in suburbia in 1959. Write a diary entry describing a typical day in your life, remembering to include fads or entertainments.

3. The so-called baby-boomers as a group have had a tremendous impact on life in the United States. Both government and industry have made in the past and are currently making projections into the future about the needs of this demographic group. Use as a base of reference a generation of baby-boomers born in 1946. Divide the class into six groups assigning each to a decade: 1950-1959, 1960-1969, 1970-1979, 1980-1989, 1990-1999,

2010-2019. (Omit 2000-2009, since these projections are very short term.) Encourage students to consult the *Reader's Guide to Periodical Literature* for sources. Ask students to research either the historical impact or the projected impact of these baby-boomers in the areas of medical care, housing, clothing, education, old-age benefits, and entertainment/leisure pursuits during their assigned decade. Ask each group to make an oral presentation about its decade to the class using a variety of media to illustrate its findings.

4. Extended activity: History often exhibits a cyclical nature. Ask several students to compare the 1920s, 1950s, and 1980s for common attributes in such areas as politics, economics, religion, social patterns, intellectual thought, the arts, and popular culture. Ask them to share their findings with the class through oral presentations.

Exercise 1: Social History and Popular Culture

Worksheet 1

Directions: Use information from document 5 to complete the worksheet.

1. How many children were being born in the United States each month?

   _____

   _____

2. How many more schools were needed to meet the baby boom?
   How much would they cost?

   _____

   _____

3. How much was the demand for electrical energy expected to increase by 1975?

   _____

   _____

4. Give at least two reasons why the United States needed more roads.

   _____

   _____

5. How has employment changed since 1939?

   _____

   _____

6. Give two reasons why Americans had more leisure time.

   _____

   _____

7. What is the Advertising Council?

   _____

   _____

I

8. How did the people who wrote the pamphlet feel about America's future?

_____

_____

9. What items about this pamphlet suggest the time period in which it was written?

_____

_____

10. What can you find out about the popular image of family from this pamphlet?

_____

_____

11. Why do you think this pamphlet was written? Is there any evidence of bias or one-sided information?

_____

_____

Exercise 2
McCarthyism and an Atmosphere of Distrust

Note to the Teacher:

The Eisenhower administration, like Truman's before it, was preoccupied with the possibility of security risks. It believed that Soviet espionage agents and traitorous American Communists could be contained by tightening security requirements. Prominent members of Congress kept the issue visible before the public by continued congressional probes of alleged Communist infiltration of the government. The two most influential of the investigating committees were the House Un-American Activities Committee and the Internal Security Subcommittee of the Senate Government Operations Committee.

No one was above suspicion. Even Lucille Ball, the popular madcap television comedienne, had to defend herself at a House hearing in 1953. Being tainted "red" had ruined many other entertainment personalities before her, from singer Paul Robeson to lyricist Yip Harburg (best known for the movie *The Wizard of Oz*). Thus, it was an impassioned defense that Lucy's husband, Desi Arnaz, offered. "Lucille Ball's no Communist. Lucy has never been a Communist, not now and never will be. I was kicked out of Cuba because of Communism. We both despise Communists and everything they stand for. Lucille Ball is one hundred percent American. She's as American as Barney Baruch and Ike Eisenhower. Please, ladies and gentlemen, don't believe every piece of bunk you read in today's papers.... And now, I want you to meet my favorite wife — my favorite redhead — in fact, that's the only thing red about her, and even that's not legitimate!" [For documents related to the investigation of Lucille Ball, check the FBI's Web Site: **FOIA.FBI.gov/ball**.]

However, the man whose name became synonymous with the era was Senator Joseph R. McCarthy of Wisconsin, chairman of the Senate Internal Security Subcommittee, who is pictured in **document 6**. Through sensational accusations, fabricated evidence, guilt by association, secret denunciation, and blacklisting, he had become one of the most powerful men in Washington, DC. Eisenhower believed that McCarthy was an embarrassment and would destroy himself if left alone. But McCarthy's November 24, 1953, televised attack on Eisenhower's State Department forced Eisenhower to take moderate action. Almost daily, through releases to the media by Press Secretary Hagerty or congressional allies, the administration condemned the types of action in which McCarthy engaged, although he was not mentioned by name. He was, nevertheless, demoted by his colleagues through reassignment to another subcommittee of the Senate's obscure Government Relations Committee.

Undaunted, McCarthy pursued his investigations, and in the spring of 1954 he attacked the army. In his May 17, 1954, letter to Secretary of Defense Charles Wilson, Eisenhower identified the constitutional separation of powers and executive privilege as a means of curtailing McCarthy. "Because it is essential to efficient and effective administration that employees of the Executive Branch be in a position to be completely candid in advising each other on official matters, and because it is not in the public interest that any of their conversations or communications, or any documents or reproductions concerning such advice be disclosed, you will instruct employees of your Department that in all of their appearances before the Subcommittee of the Senate Committee on Government Operations regarding the inquiry now before it they are not to testify to any such conversations or communications or to produce any such documents or reproductions."

When the army revealed that McCarthy had sought favors for his aide David Schine, who was drafted into the army in 1953, McCarthy demanded the hearings be televised. For 36 days, Americans watched McCarthy browbeat and insult witnesses and interrupt testimony with parliamentary procedures,

2

constantly insisting on "point of order." On June 9, 1954, McCarthy launched into accusations about the integrity of a young aide to the army's attorney, Joseph Welch. This exchange is contained in **sound recording A**. Welch's reply so moved onlookers that they ignored the rules of conduct at a committee hearing to applaud Welch.

McCarthy finally had destroyed himself, as he had destroyed the lives of thousands of U.S. citizens. Later that fall he was censured by the Senate for procedural irregularities and insulting witnesses. His power gone, he faded away and died in 1957, a broken man.

Time: 1 to 2 class periods

Objectives:

- To analyze the techniques of McCarthyism.

- To evaluate the impact of the media on a historical event.

- To develop listening skills.

Materials Needed:

Documents 6, 30
Sound recording A
Sound Recording Analysis worksheet, p. 15

Procedures:

1. Duplicate the Sound Recording Analysis worksheet and distribute a copy to each student. Play sound recording A to the entire class. After the students complete the worksheet, review it and discuss questions your students may raise.

2. Ask students to describe the image they have formed of McCarthy based on the auditory information alone. Pass document 6 around to the class so each student gets a chance to look at it. Pose the following questions to students for discussion:

   a. Is there a difference between having a picture of a person while listening to his or her voice and having an auditory impression alone? If so, what is it?

   b. How does the effect of television coverage of an event contrast with that of radio coverage of the same event?

   c. What effect has media coverage had on national events? Cite examples of significant instances in which media coverage of an event may have altered its outcome.

   d. How did television coverage contribute to McCarthy's demise?

   e. Do you think that people use the media today to attack other people unfairly? How can people respond to public accusation?

   f. Discuss the inherent tension between freedom of speech/press and the right to privacy.

3. The term McCarthyism has become synonymous with a reckless and unsupported attack against people by use of techniques such as guilt by association, imposition of loyalty oaths, scrutiny by secret informants, blacklists, suppression of citizens' freedoms of speech and assembly, interrogation and intimidation of the accused by public committees, and submission of unsupported allegations against the accused. Ask students to define these techniques. Play sound recording A again and ask the students to list examples of these techniques. When students have completed making their notes, ask them to share their findings as a class. Invite students to consider whether, if McCarthy had been able to identify Communist activists in the government, the ends would have justified the means.

4. Extended activity: Ask students to examine earlier periods in U.S. history when Americans were obsessed with malign influences. The students should compare and contrast the atmosphere and methods of McCarthyism in the 1950s with that of the Red Scare of the 1920s, the ante bellum Know-Nothing movement, and the 1692 Salem witch trials. Ask students to share their findings through oral or written reports.

Exercise 3
Black Civil Rights

Note to the Teacher:

In the 1950s the move to secure full civil rights for black Americans gained momentum through the actions of all three branches of the federal government and through the prodding of the National Association for the Advancement of Colored People (NAACP). Since the mid-30s the NAACP had lobbied and litigated in an effort to overturn the "separate but equal" doctrine enunciated in the *Plessy v. Ferguson* decision by the Supreme Court in 1896. That case had involved only the question of whether blacks could be barred by the state of Louisiana from riding in white-occupied railroad cars, but its principle was applied and extended especially in the South to other social areas as well, most significantly to education.

Before l951 there had been no direct challenge to elementary and secondary school racial segregation. A change began in that year when Oliver Brown sued the Topeka, KS, school board to allow his 8-year-old daughter to attend a white public school located nearby. After lower federal courts rejected his suit, Brown, with the help of the NAACP, appealed to the Supreme Court.

Adding later school desegregation cases to Brown's, the Court ruled on May 17, 1954, that "separate educational facilities are inherently unequal" and that such facilities had no place in public education. Racial discrimination in public education was unconstitutional under the provisions of the 14th Amendment's equal protection clause.

This landmark decision eventually paved the way for the destruction of legalized educational segregation. A year later the Court ordered that desegregation be carried out under lower federal court direction "with all deliberate speed." **Document 7** is an order to the district court of Kansas.

It was ultimately up to the executive branch to enforce the Court's desegregation rulings, but President Eisenhower was reluctant to press for compliance too aggressively. "I don't believe you can change the hearts of men with laws or decisions," he once observed; yet it was Eisenhower who mandated the swift desegregation of Washington, DC, schools as a model for the rest of the country. He hoped that most states would voluntarily comply with the spirit as well as the letter of the law and proceed quickly in the matter.

However, attempts to desegregate often met fierce resistance, particularly from those southern states that disagreed with the Court that integration of educational facilities was required. Since neither the Constitution's original articles nor its amendments, including the 14th, explicitly mentioned education as a matter of federal control, and since under the Constitution powers not given to the federal government are reserved to the states, these states believed that they were free to maintain segregated school systems as they wished without federal interference.

One state that initially would not comply with the Supreme Court's ruling was Arkansas. In 1957, defiant Governor Orval Faubus ordered national guardsmen to block the entry of nine black students to Little Rock's Central High School. As a former military officer, President Eisenhower knew that such resistance could not be tolerated and thereupon federalized the guard. For the first time since Reconstruction, a U.S. President ordered federal troops to defend the rights of black citizens. **Document 8** is the text of the President's address to the nation explaining his action.

Initially, the legislative branch was slow to respond to the need for laws expanding black rights out of fear that such actions might prove unpopular with white constituents, especially in the South. Democratic Party leaders in the House and Senate did not want to jeopardize the party majority in both

Houses, which coalition on other issues had created. Vigorous action on behalf of civil rights legislation threatened to cause a permanent split. However, under the able Senate Majority Leader Lyndon B. Johnson (see document 35 for photograph), the first civil rights bill in 72 years was passed in 1957. This landmark bill (document 9) provided for the establishment of the Civil Rights Commission and proposed the enactment of laws for the protection of voting rights. Document 10 is the report of the Committee on the Judiciary, which accompanied H.R. 6127.

Angered by the slowness of government response to the NAACP's legal and legislative campaigns, a new generation of black leaders sprang up. These individuals and their followers favored more confrontational, direct approaches of the sort employed in Montgomery, AL, when blacks boycotted the bus system in protest over segregated seating. Rev. Dr. Martin Luther King, Jr., emerged from that boycott a national figure and the recognized spokesman for nonviolent civil disobedience as evidenced by his appearance on "Meet the Press" in 1960 and recorded in **sound recording B**.

Nonviolent civil disobedience took many forms, such as sit-ins, economic boycotts, and street demonstrations. **Document 11** is a memo regarding the strategy of sit-ins. Peaceful as they were, many civil rights activists endured beatings, racial taunts, and brutal arrests in many southern cities. As other Americans saw the protests on television and in the newspapers, many resolved to join in the fight, requesting legislative and executive remedies to right these wrongs. **Document 12** is a resolution by the United Postal Workers of America urging the President and Congress to investigate the "denial of basic democratic and social rights to the millions of American Negroes living in [the South]."

Time: 1 to 3 class periods

Objectives:

- To assess the impact of the civil rights movement on U.S. life.

- To consider the effects of segregation and desegregation on Americans.

- To determine the chronology of the postwar civil rights movement.

Materials Needed:

Documents 7-12, 35
Sound recording B
Written Document Analysis worksheet, p. 13
Worksheet 2

Procedures:

1. Review the content of document 10 using the Written Document Analysis worksheet.

2. Duplicate and distribute documents 7-12 and worksheet 2. Play sound recording B for the students. Ask students to review the documents along with the section on civil rights in their textbooks, then answer the questions and complete the time line. After students complete the worksheet, review it and discuss questions your students may raise.

3. Conduct a role-play exercise with the students. Begin by establishing a situation of tension between two Little Rock Central High School students — one black and one white. Ask two students to come to the front of the classroom, assign the roles, and create a situation.

For example, the scene may take place in the classroom where the white student objects to the black student sitting next to him or her. The white student says.... Continue the scene for a few minutes between the two students, then gradually add more pressure roles to the situation, changing the setting when appropriate. You might add a teacher, another student, a principal, a parent, a school board member, an "agitator," or a government official. Add no more than four additional roles. When the pressure peaks, stop the scene. Lead a discussion with the class asking the participants about the effects the pressure had on each of them. Ask the class to determine the extent of the tension and to relate this tension to the real situations in Little Rock, Montgomery, Greensboro, and other sites of desegregation conflict.

4. Ask students to consider if it is possible to "change the hearts of men with laws." Ask them how they would have dealt with this issue. Try to establish several possible responses to the fact of discrimination in the 1950s.

FOR RELEASE AT 9:00 P.M. EDT, SEPTEMBER 24, 1957

James C. Hagerty, Press Secretary to the President

- -

THE WHITE HOUSE

TEXT OF THE ADDRESS BY THE PRESIDENT
OF THE UNITED STATES, DELIVERED FROM
HIS OFFICE AT THE WHITE HOUSE, TUESDAY,
SEPTEMBER 24, 1957, AT 9:00 P.M. EDT

My Fellow Citizens:

For a few minutes I want to speak to you about the serious situation that has arisen in Little Rock. For this talk I have come to the President's office in the White House. I could have spoken from Rhode Island, but I felt that, in speaking from the house of Lincoln, of Jackson and of Wilson, my words would more clearly convey both the sadness I feel in the action I was compelled today to take and the firmness with which I intend to pursue this course until the orders of the Federal Court at Little Rock can be executed without unlawful interference.

In that city, under the leadership of demagogic extremists, disorderly mobs have deliberately prevented the carrying out of proper orders from a Federal Court. Local authorities have not eliminated that violent opposition and, under the law, I yesterday issued a Proclamation calling upon the mob to disperse.

This morning the mob again gathered in front of the Central High School of Little Rock, obviously for the purpose of again preventing the carrying out of the Court's order relating to the admission of Negro children to the school.

Whenever normal agencies prove inadequate to the task and it becomes necessary for the Executive Branch of the Federal Government to use its powers and authority to uphold Federal Courts, the President's responsibility is inescapable.

In accordance with that responsibility, I have today issued an Executive Order directing the use of troops under Federal authority to aid in the execution of Federal law at Little Rock, Arkansas. This became necessary when my Proclamation of yesterday was not observed, and the obstruction of justice still continues.

It is important that the reasons for my action be understood by all citizens.

As you know, the Supreme Court of the United States has decided that separate public educational facilities for the races are inherently unequal and therefore compulsory school segregation laws are unconstitutional.

more

Exercise 3: Black Civil Rights

Worksheet 2

Directions: Study documents 7-12, sound recording B, and your textbook to answer the questions and complete the time line.

1. Which document shows the role of the black community in promoting civil change?

   _____

2. Which document shows the role of the legislative branch in promoting civil change?

   _____

3. Which document shows the role of the executive branch in promoting civil change?

   _____

4. Which document shows the role of the judicial branch in promoting civil change?

   _____

5. Which document shows the role of the private sector in promoting civil change?

   _____

6. What single piece of information in these documents was the most surprising to you? Copy the sentence.

   _____

   _____

   What is your reaction to it?

   _____

7. What is the purpose of the sit-in technique? How effective is it?

   _____

   _____

3

8. What is the purpose of the resolution? How effective is it?

_____

_____

9. Through what means does Congress ensure compliance to laws it passes?

_____

_____

_____

10. Indicate where each document fits on this time line, then add major events of the civil rights movement to complete the time line.

1954

1955

1956

1957

1958

1959

1960

Exercise 4
Science and Technology: Progress and Apprehension

Note to the Teacher:

Throughout the postwar period, science and technology generally were held in a type of esteem usually reserved for religion. There was a euphoric confidence in the ability of the human mind to discover answers to all questions and to devise inventions to end all problems. Natural and organic approaches were discarded in favor of scientific and synthetic ones, from fertilizers to fabrics. Scientists talked of controlling the weather by 1976.

Certainly there were triumphs. The spectre of wheelchairs and iron lung machines was dispelled by the development of a polio vaccine by Dr. Jonas Salk, who is pictured in **document 13**. Over 1.8 million school children were vaccinated in 1954 during the largest medical field test in history. The successful test results led to the passage of the Poliomyelitis Vaccination Act of 1955. Over the objections of the Eisenhower administration that this legislation would lead to socialized medicine, Congress allocated $30 million to be disbursed by the Public Health Service to the states to purchase polio vaccine.

The United States pursued testing of nuclear weapons, confident that deterrence through strength would ensure peace. Most scientists were certain that they knew all the dangers of exposure to nuclear energy and permitted troops to be trained at test sites, such as Yucca Flats, as reported in **sound recording C** by Charles Collingwood for CBS. But the United States had no monopoly on scientific progress. The Soviets' 1957 success with *Sputnik* galled Americans. In **document 14**, administration spokesmen rationalized that the United States was not behind in the space race. Although the Russians could lift heavier objects, Americans had more varied and sophisticated space technology. For example, America's first Earth satellite, *Explorer 1*, launched on January 31, 1958, was only the size of a grapefruit, but it had the technical capacity to conduct experiments that discovered the Van Allen radiation belt.

There was a darker side to progress that most Americans sensed. Although the few Quakers and pacifists who opposed the atom bomb were dismissed as eccentrics or Communist sympathizers, many people worried about the possibility of atomic war. This anxiety is conveyed by a civil defense poster of the time, **document 15**. Was space — the great unknown — friendly, neutral, or hostile? The U.S. Air Force entertained the possibility that extraterrestrials existed and maintained reports of sightings of unidentified flying objects (UFOs) in Project Blue Book, an example of which is found in **document 16**. Nonetheless, the attitude of the time was best expressed by the subtitle of the 1964 film *Dr. Strangelove: How I Learned to Stop Worrying and Love the Bomb*.

Time: 1-2 periods

Objectives:

*   To describe scientific and technological advances of the 1950s.

*   To apply a decision-making model to historic and current decisions.

4

Materials Needed:

Documents 13-16
Sound recording C
Photograph Analysis worksheet, p. 14
Worksheet 3

Procedures:

1. Duplicate document 13 and the Photograph Analysis worksheet and distribute a copy of each to every student. After students have completed the assignment, answer questions they might have.

2. Duplicate and distribute documents 15 and 16 and ask students to examine them closely. Ask students to share their initial reactions to the documents. Play sound recording C for the students and discuss their reactions to its content and tone. Ask students to select one of the following roles and write a paragraph reacting to information found in the related document.

   a. You were the pilot experiencing the sighting of the UFO.
   b. You were a 1954 school child viewing the civil defense poster.
   c. You were a soldier at Yucca Flats.

3. Divide the class into six groups and hand out copies of document 14 for each group. Instruct students to examine the document carefully and answer the following questions.

   a. Why has the exploration of space been called a "space race"? What effect did the concept of space exploration as a "race" have upon the subsequent exploration of space?
   b. What scientific benefits come from manned space exploration? What publicity benefits come from manned space exploration?
   c. Has NASA sacrificed quality in a rush to keep ahead?
   d. How did our system of government facilitate our efforts to compete with the Soviets in space? How did our system complicate our efforts to compete with the Soviets in space?

4. The following procedure was adapted from an exercise developed for the Teacher in Space project, Mission 51-L, the space shuttle mission carrying Christa McAuliffe and the crew of *Challenger*, which so tragically ended on January 28, 1986.

   Using the Spaceship Decision-making Model on worksheet 3, apply the model to a variety of space-oriented problems. Individual students or small groups should select one historical, present, or future space-oriented problem. Ask them to research the problem and alternatives available for its solution. Using the model, ask students to weigh the benefits and costs, then make a decision. Ask them to outline their decision-making steps, concluding with their decision and reasoning, and to turn it in. Compare the historic decisions with the students' decisions and discuss why they were similar or dissimilar, and whether the outcome would have been different if a different decision had been made.

a. Historical Decisions

1) Creation of NASA

2) Establishment of Kennedy's goal of reaching the moon before 1970

3) Participation of other countries in early space efforts

4) Continuation of Apollo program after 1967 deaths

5) Inclusion of women as astronauts

6) Launching of *Apollo/Soyuz* joint mission

b. Current Decisions

1) Sharing scientific data with other nations

2) Use of Earth observation satellite data by governments

3) Dispersal of tax moneys on space exploration rather than other budget items

4) Launching of manned v. unmanned space missions

5) Development and deployment of Strategic Defense Initiative ("Star Wars")

c. Future Decisions

1) Space colonization

2) Space manufacturing or mining facilities

3) International space ventures

4) Exploring other planets

5. Extended activity: Movies and novels have dealt with both the fears and triumphs of 20th-century science. Some science fiction books and films have been filled with atomic holocaust and mutant monsters, from *Canticle for Leibowitz* to *Godzilla*. Others have celebrated the bold exploration of astronauts, such as *The Right Stuff*.

Ask students to select 10 titles from 1950-2000 science fiction for either a recommended reading list or a recommended viewing list, writing a justification for each title selected.

4

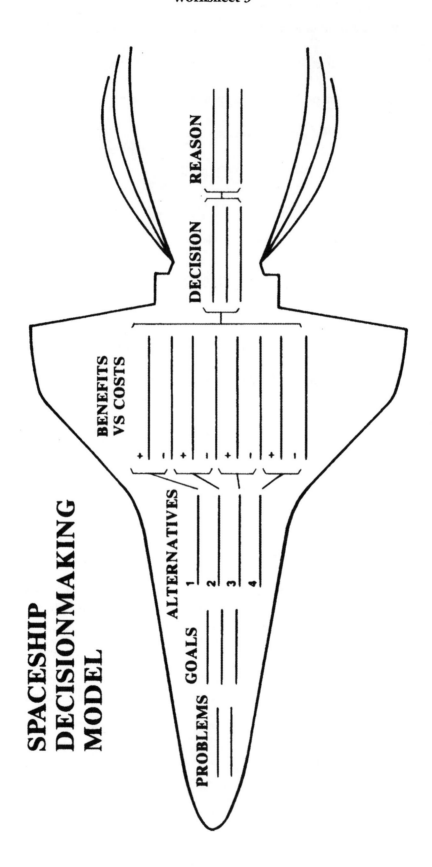

SPACESHIP DECISIONMAKING MODEL

Exercise 5
United States and Soviet Relations

Note to the Teacher:

Relations between the United States and the Soviet Union dominated foreign affairs during the Eisenhower Presidency. Despite the bitter divisions between the two sides, opportunity for a thaw in the cold war appeared toward the end of Eisenhower's second term.

Mutual suspicion had been mounting between the two superpowers since World War II, but the Geneva summit of 1955 began to ease the tension. Reluctant to agree to substantive arms control at that summit, the Soviets did agree to a cultural exchange. One of the most notable of these exchanges was young Van Cliburn's participation in an international piano competition in Moscow, where he took first place. **Document 17** is a photograph of Cliburn and the President after Cliburn's success abroad.

This cultural exchange culminated in a Soviet exhibition in New York and a U.S. exhibition in Moscow. President Eisenhower gave Vice President Richard Nixon a message to deliver to Soviet Premier Nikita Khrushchev when he attended the Moscow exhibition in July 1959. **Document 18** is Khrushchev's reply. The Vice President, accompanied by Khrushchev, visited the U.S. exhibition. As they ambled through the exhibition's model kitchens, surrounded by reporters, the two leaders clashed in a widely publicized verbal encounter later dubbed "the kitchen debate," a part of which can be heard on **sound recording D**.

At the time of Nixon's visit, President Eisenhower invited Premier Khrushchev to visit the United States. Khrushchev arrived in mid-September for a 10-day visit. **Document 19** is a five-page memo outlining U.S. objectives for the meeting. President Eisenhower had hoped to persuade Khrushchev that by helping to improve the international climate he could gain a place in history. Although little of substance emerged from the meeting, plans were made by the two heads of state to meet again in Paris in May 1960. Thereafter, President Eisenhower and his family would proceed to the Soviet Union for a visit. Never in the cold war had the prospects for a real agreement seemed more possible. Khrushchev returned home speaking warmly of the "spirit of Camp David," and Eisenhower looked forward to a breakthrough in the arms race as his final act as a world leader.

Unfortunately that opportunity never came for Eisenhower. On the eve of the Paris summit, a U.S. U-2 reconnaissance plane was shot down over Soviet territory. Eisenhower believed that neither the plane nor the pilot could have survived. Seeking to protect the secrecy of intelligence-gathering overflights, he decided to lie about the mission, insisting that it was a "weather research" plane. Two days later, the Soviets announced that not only had they recovered the plane but also the pilot. **Document 20** is a photograph of a bulletin board in Moscow displaying the evidence of the incident to the Soviet people.

Amid this rapidly deteriorating scenario, the world leaders gathered in Paris for the summit. At the initial meeting, Khrushchev launched into a tirade against Eisenhower and the United States, ending by announcing that Eisenhower was no longer welcome in the Soviet Union. Then he and the entire Soviet delegation stalked out. **Document 21** is a special staff note detailing how the U.S. Information Agency planned to explain the canceled summit to the rest of the world.

Time: 1 to 2 class periods

5

Objectives:

- To examine the relationship between the United States and the Soviet Union during the 1950s.

- To read for facts and general content.

- To identify and evaluate arguments and to formulate a position on an issue.

Materials Needed:

Documents 17-21
Sound recording D
Worksheet 4

Procedures:

1. Many terms mentioned in these documents need to be identified for students. Duplicate and distribute document 19 and ask the students to locate the following terms in the memorandum: balance of power, Soviet bloc, arms limitation, peaceful coexistence, "Foreign Affairs," bilateral relations, remilitarization, summit conference, and Camp David. Also, ask students to identify cold war, U-2, and reconnaissance. Using the resources in the classroom (textbooks and reference books), ask students to explain each term.

2. Duplicate documents 17-21 and provide each group of 3-4 students with a set of copies. Instruct students to examine the documents and carefully listen to sound recording D in order to answer the following questions:
   a. What can you tell about the personality of Eisenhower from the content, emphasis, style, and/or wording of these documents?
   b. What can you tell about the personality of Khrushchev from the content, emphasis, style, and/or wording of these documents?
   c. What can you tell about the personality of Nixon from the content, emphasis, style, and/or wording of these documents?
   d. How can different personalities interact? What are some of the consequences?

3. Duplicate and distribute worksheet 4. Instruct students to search in their textbook and library for data on summits between the two nations since the May 1960 Paris Summit Conference.

4. Extended activity: Ask students to select one of the following issues and to write a short paper in which they formulate a position on the issue and include at least three supporting pieces of evidence. The issues are as follows:
   a. Should journalists publicize classified information?
   b. Are there instances when the government is justified in disseminating untruths? What are some recent examples of this and what has been their effect on policy and on the public?
   c. Is espionage ethical?
   d. Is counterespionage ethical?
   e. Is intelligence gathering ethical?
   f. Should government officials "leak" classified information to the press when the government benefits from such leaks? Should government officials "leak" classified information to the press when the government is embarrassed by such disclosure?

Exercise 5: United States and Soviet Relations

Worksheet 4

Date/Location	Who were the personalities/ heads of state?	What were the purposes of the meeting?	What was accomplished?

Exercise 6
The Far East: Korea and Vietnam

Note to the Teacher:

In the Far East, President Eisenhower oversaw the end of one conflict and the beginning of another. One of the first tasks of the new President was to end the Korean war. By April 1953 the North Koreans had agreed to resume armistice talks at Panmunjom, but the President found that he had important negotiating to do on his own side of the bargaining table. Secretary of State John Foster Dulles and South Korean President Syngman Rhee were pressing for the reunification of Korea rather than a mere armistice at the 38th parallel. Eisenhower realized that an all-out war in the nuclear age was unthinkable but that the limited war we had been fighting was unwinnable, so he stood firm against Dulles and cajoled Rhee into a final acceptance of the armistice. **Document 22** is the text of the statement the President made to the nation shortly after the armistice was signed. One of the major negotiating hurdles was whether prisoners of war (POW) should be repatriated automatically, as the North Koreans insisted, or voluntarily, as the United Nations wanted. **Document 23** shows a letter to the President from the mother of a POW. The United States continued to have close ties with South Korea after the armistice was concluded, as **document 24**, a mutual defense treaty, indicates.

Meanwhile the United States was becoming more deeply involved in Vietnam. At the end of World War II, the United States had urged the French to relinquish their colonial rule in Vietnam. Fearful that other important colonies, most notably oil-rich Algeria, might also demand their independence, the French held on to Vietnam believing that they could defeat the opposition forces led by Ho Chi Minh. As that conflict continued into the 1950s, the United States faced a dilemma. It did not want to support a colonial power, but failure to do so would have led to the success of Ho Chi Minh, who was not only a nationalist whose popularity extended throughout his country, but also a Communist. Eisenhower later wrote in his memoirs, "The standing of the United States as the most powerful of the anti-colonial powers is an asset of incalculable value to the free world." Nonetheless, Eisenhower and Dulles decided to support the French financially, and by 1954 military aid to the French had reached amounts of one billion dollars a year. In April 1954 the French, surrounded by the Viet Minh at Dien Bien Phu in the northern part of Vietnam, appealed to the United States for support troops. Eisenhower refused. In May 1954 the Joint Chiefs of Staff wrote "A Concept for Action with Regard to Indochina" **(document 25)**.

The Geneva Accords, signed in July 1954, established a cease-fire between the French and the Viet Minh, provided for the temporary division of Vietnam into North Vietnam and South Vietnam, for the withdrawal of French troops, and called for nationwide elections by 1956. The United States did not sign the agreement, fearing that free elections would lead to the election of Ho Chi Minh. Instead the United States supported a government in South Vietnam led first by Bao Dai and then by Ngo Dinh Diem. In 1960, Diem and President Eisenhower exchanged letters **(document 26)** on the occasion of the anniversary of a free South Vietnam. Diem continued to rule South Vietnam until 1963, when he was assassinated in a coup.

The division of Vietnam and its subsequent civil war led to the displacement of large numbers of Vietnamese. As early as the summer of 1954, vast numbers of refugees were moving from north to south. **Document 27** is a report of the refugee movement.

Time: 1 to 2 class periods

Objectives:

- To describe U.S. policies in the Far East following World War II.

- To examine the forming of public opinion to support policies.

- To compare and contrast the Korean war and the Vietnamese war.

Materials Needed:

Documents 22-27
Worksheet 5

Procedures:

1. Duplicate and distribute documents 22-24 and worksheet 5. After the students have completed the questions, discuss the worksheet with the class.

2. On April 7, 1954, at a news conference, Eisenhower introduced the "domino theory" while commenting on the strategic importance of Indochina. "You have a row of dominoes set up, you knock over the first one, and what will happen to the last one is the certainty that it will go over very quickly. So you could have a beginning of a disintegration that would have the most profound influences." As a class, consider the following questions:

   a. What countries of Southeast Asia were thought to be threatened?

   b. What countries of the western Pacific could be at risk if Southeast Asia fell?

   c. Has the "domino theory" been borne out in Southeast Asia?

   d. Eisenhower also feared a domino effect in Central America if Guatemala fell to communism. What countries would be threatened?

   e. Eisenhower feared a domino effect if the islands off the coast of China, Quemoy and Matsu, fell to the Chinese Communists. What countries were at risk?

   f. Is the "domino theory" a valid theory today?

3. Duplicate and distribute documents 25-27. Ask students to list techniques the United States used to mold public opinion in Vietnam and the world at large in favor of U.S. opposition to Ho Chi Minh. Tell the students that in 1946 Ho Chi Minh urged, "Whoever you may be, men, women, children, old or young, whatever your religion or whatever your nationality, if you are Vietnamese, rise up to fight the French colonialists, to save our country." Then ask them what approaches Ho Chi Minh used to mold public opinion in Vietnam and the world at large to oppose U.S. support of the French and then South Vietnamese governments.

4. Extended activity: Ask students to compare the Korean war and the Vietnam war. They should consider a number of points. Are they typical of civil wars? What was the significance of a dividing line (e.g., North Korea and South Korea)? What refugee problems were there? How were civilian populations used? What was the effect on civilian populations? How was the prisoner-of-war issue handled? What was the role of the United States, China, the Soviet Union, and the United Nations in each case? How does each of these conflicts fit the policy of containment?

6

Exercise 6: The Far East

Worksheet 5

Directions: Study documents 22-24 carefully. Check either "True" or "False" in the column to the left of each statement.

True   **False**

_____   _____   1. There were 17 other nations that fought in Korea along with the United States.

_____   _____   2. Prisoners of war were all returned without review.

_____   _____   3. A permanent peace was not achieved in Korea.

_____   _____   4. Korea was not unified after the armistice.

_____   _____   5. The United States and the Republic of Korea agreed to defend each other.

_____   _____   6. The mutual defense treaty between the United States and the Republic of Korea entered into force when it was signed.

_____   _____   7. The Senate advises the President whether or not to ratify a treaty.

_____   _____   8. Lt. Barney Cummings became a prisoner-of-war in August 1950.

_____   _____   9. The prisoner-of-war exchange continued indefinitely.

_____   _____   10. The North Koreans sometimes released photographs to the Associated Press.

Exercise 7
Trouble Spots

Note to the Teacher:

As the cold war lengthened, the superpowers had to take into account a crucial new factor — emerging nationalism. Although the United States and the Soviet Union continued to do verbal battle during the Eisenhower administration, both sides began to reject war. Rather than risk nuclear holocaust, they opted for waging war by proxy. Working behind the scenes in countries currently undergoing revolution or ripe for it, the Soviet Union and the United States each sought to erode the other's influence politically and militarily and to enhance its own. For the United States, this often entailed covert action by the Central Intelligence Agency (CIA) to foment or forestall change in nations seen to be of strategic or other importance.

The United States feared that Communist agitators would subvert indigenous nationalistic movements taking place in both Iran and Guatemala. In the former, the CIA worked in 1953 to create opposition to a coalition led by Prime Minister Mohammed Mossadegh. Mossadegh and his allies (which included the Tudeh, or Iranian Communist Party, the Moslem clergy, and extreme nationalists) had successfully nationalized British-held oil properties and unseated Shah Mohammed Reza Pahlavi, the existing ruler. The Shah had upheld British and U.S. interests, and therefore his restoration to power was something very much desired by those powers.

The CIA developed Operation Ajax to restore the Shah. Under the leadership of Kermit Roosevelt, the CIA bribed key Iranian army officers, orchestrated pro-Shah street demonstrations, and on August 22, 1953, Fazlollah Zahedi, a pro-Shah general supported by the United States, led the Iranian army in a coup that enabled the Shah to return. Mossadegh and other extremists were placed under arrest and jailed, and a grateful Shah negotiated a new oil export agreement ensuring 40 percent of the oil for the United States. **Document 28**, from 1958, indicates U.S. concern over the long-term stability of the Shah's regime.

Closer to home, the United States worried about the consequences of the land reform program conducted in 1954 under Guatemala's leftist president, Jacobo Arbenz Guzman. This reform movement, as well intended as it was in attacking the problem of unequal distribution of wealth that was destabilizing the region, appeared to U.S. policy strategists to jeopardize the sizable financial interests of the U.S. firm United Fruit Company; even worse, it seemed to invite government takeover by the Communists. If this happened, it was feared Guatemala would become a base from which to export larger hemispheric revolution, and the nations of Central America might collapse like dominoes. To meet this perceived threat, the CIA launched Operation Pbsuccess, modeled after Operation Ajax in Iran, to turn the Guatemalan army against Arbenz and cause a coup. Arbenz decided to arm his people's militia to compensate for the army's defection.

Support for Arbenz from the Soviet bloc moved the United States to action. On May 15, 1953, the *Alfhem*, a Swedish merchant vessel, docked in Guatemala with a cargo for Arbenz, including light arms from Czechoslovakia. John Foster Dulles denounced the shipment as a violation of the Monroe Doctrine. Eisenhower ordered an airlift of weapons to neighboring anti-Communist regimes in Nicaragua and Honduras to help them resist Communist aggression. He also announced a naval blockade and the intent to search a ship in Hamburg, Germany, suspected of carrying a shipment of Soviet weapons for Arbenz. Anti-Arbenz rebel Castillo Armas, backed by the United States, launched an attack from Honduras, but attracted little popular support. The United States provided two P-51 aircraft to Nicaraguan dictator Anastasio Samoza, who passed them on to Armas. Armas was further supported by CIA pilots who flew bombing raids on Guatemala City from their bases in Managua, Nicaragua. Following

7

these bombing raids and his failure to convince the U.N. Security Council to send observers, Arbenz was forced to resign. By June 30, 1954, the Guatemalan army was in charge of the country.

In 1960 Guatemala and Nicaragua requested U.S. naval patrols to prevent Cuban Communist ruler Fidel Castro from sending in forces to overthrow their governments. **Document 29** is a White House translation of a telegram from the Guatemalan President thanking Eisenhower for the United States' help.

In late 1956, a pair of events occurred that shook both the U.S.-created NATO and the Soviet-created Warsaw Pact alliances. Since 1952, the United States had incited agitation in the satellites of the Soviet Union as indicated in **document 30**. Nonetheless, U.S. policy was geared to contain communism in Eastern Europe rather than to liberate the countries in that part of the world. Thus, when the people of Hungary began to demand changes in their government, the United States was not prepared to provide more than moral and verbal support for the dissidents in an area acknowledged to be within the Soviet sphere of influence.

Initial restlessness with the brand of communism rigidly subscribed to by Moscow led to the Hungarian government's appointment on October 23, 1956, of a more progressive Hungarian Prime Minister, Imre Nagy. When rioting continued, Stalinist Communist Party Chief Gero invited the Soviet Union to send in troops to quell the disturbance. Hungarian progressives then sought assistance from the United States, while the CIA requested permission to provide arms and supplies in their support. However, Hungary was isolated, lacking a seaport or an approach through territory of NATO allies. The only military options available were the airlift of supplies long distances over hostile territory at the risk of U.S. lives or the use of atomic weapons. Eisenhower would not plunge the world into a nuclear war to help the Hungarian freedom fighters. So, they stood alone on October 24 with homemade Molotov cocktails to repel the 10,000 Soviet troops and 80 tanks that entered Budapest. They resisted unrelentingly and valiantly, sometimes successfully seizing Soviet tanks, as photographed in **document 31**. On October 31, the Russians announced that they would withdraw.

At almost the same time that nationalistic fervor was feeding resistance in Hungary, it was fueling a similar fire in the Middle East. On October 29 Israel attacked Egypt, invading the Sinai Peninsula to retaliate against numerous Egyptian raids into Israeli territory. Israel's action took advantage of the furor over Egyptian President Gamal Abdel Nasser's decision to nationalize the foreign-built Suez Canal. Two days later, Great Britain joined the assault, bombing Egypt in an effort to discredit Nasser's leadership. The British and French had decided to seize control of the canal, mapped in **document 32**, but on October 31, Eisenhower refused to assist the joint Anglo-French force that was poised to invade Egypt for that purpose. Instead, he reaffirmed the 1950 Tripartite Declaration that committed the United States to assist Middle Eastern victims of aggression. Eisenhower called upon the United Nations to pass a resolution insisting on a cease-fire, Israeli withdrawal from Egyptian territory, restraint of any U.N. members wishing to intervene forcibly in Egyptian affairs, and placement of U.N. peacekeeping forces in the region.

World attention distracted by the events at Suez was soon drawn back to Hungary. On November 1, Hungary withdrew from the Warsaw Pact and declared neutrality. With defection within the Hungarian army approaching 80 percent, the Soviets acted. On November 4, the Soviets sent an additional 200,000 troops and 4,000 tanks into Budapest. Before the Soviet juggernaut, 40,000 freedom fighters died and 150,000 fled. Prime Minister Nagy was given a haven in the Yugoslav Embassy. He was pledged safe conduct out of the country, but, when he left the embassy, the Russians seized, tried, and executed him. Britain and France's Suez venture precluded their assistance as NATO allies, so Hungary's pleas for western help went unanswered. A pro-Moscow hard-line regime was installed. All the United States could do was to admit 21,000 refugees immediately and introduce emergency legislation to take in more. Cardinal Josef Mindszenty was given sanctuary in the U.S. Embassy, where he would remain for years.

The Suez Crisis intensified, too, with Arab nations embargoing the sale of oil to Western Europe. In a bizarre twist, on November 5, the Soviets proposed to the United States that a joint U.S.-Soviet force be constituted and sent to intervene in the Middle East. Sensibly, the western powers agreed to a cease-fire on November 7 and withdrew from Suez by the end of December.

Time: 1 to 2 class periods

Objectives:

- To describe U.S. policies of the 1950s in response to nationalism and communism.

- To interpret information from a map.

Materials Needed:

Documents 28-32
Worksheet 6

Procedures:

1. Duplicate document 32 and worksheet 6 and distribute copies to each student. As a class, discuss the worksheet after pupils have completed the questions.
2. Duplicate documents 28-31 and distribute them to groups of 2 to 3 students. Ask students to examine the documents carefully. Share with them background information from the Note to the Teacher and other sources. Lead a discussion using the following questions as a guide.
   a. During the cold war, what was the strategic importance to the United States of Iran? of Guatemala? of Hungary?
   b. How was the United States trying to exert influence on conditions in Iran? in Guatemala? in Hungary?
   c. Were the objectives of U.S. foreign policy served by supporting the Shah? by U.S. naval intervention in Guatemala? by propaganda in Hungary?
   d. Was Guatemala an example of or departure from the Monroe Doctrine? freedom of the seas? containment?
   e. Did Iran fit into the domino theory and, if so, how? What about Guatemala? Hungary?
   f. What method of exerting influence seemed most effective to U.S. policymakers in the 1950s?
   g. From today's perspective, what method of exerting influence in the 1950s has proved to be most effective in the long run? What has proved to be the least effective? Which methods are still used?
3. Each progressive movement in the Communist bloc, in Hungary, Czechoslovakia, and Poland, has been crushed. Select 4 students to conduct research and present oral reports on the role the United States played in the progressive movements in these countries.
4. Extended activity: Ask students to research and share with the class the fates of the following figures and their nations.
   a. Anastasio Samoza and Nicaragua
   b. The Shah and Iran
   c. The Hungarian freedom fighters and Hungary

7

Exercise 7: Trouble Spots

Worksheet 6

Directions: Study the map (document 32) and answer the following questions.

1. Calculate the distance between the following locations:

   a. Suez to Port Said _____

   b. Râs el Adabya to Râs Messab _____

   c. Newport Rock Lighthouse to Station Number 133 _____

2. How long is the Great Bitter Lake? _____

3. What is a gebel? a tell? a râs? a wadi? _____

   _____

4. What types of plants could be found around El Manayif Oasis? What landmarks are located near 31° 0'N. and 32° 30'E.?

   _____

   _____

5. What is the population of Abu Sueir? What is the population of Port Ibrahim?

   _____

   _____

6. List the methods available for travel from Râs El'ish Station to El Tîna Station.

   _____

   _____

7. Why is sweet water marked? Why is undulating sand marked? Why are some areas labeled "liable to inundation?"

   _____

   _____

8. How high is Gebel Nogra? How high is the area around Prophet's Grave (near 30° 45'N. and 33° 0'E.)?

   _____

   _____

9. What can you tell about the climate, natural resources, culture, population, and land features of this area based on information in this map alone?

   _____

   _____

10. Write an account of what you would see if you were traveling from El Kubr Station to the ruined chapel north of 30° 0'N. and 33° 0'E.

_____

_____

_____

_____

_____

_____

_____

_____

_____

_____

_____

_____

_____

_____

_____

_____

_____

_____

_____

_____

Exercise 8
People and Personalities

Note to the Teacher:

As suggested in **document 33**, a cartoon highlighting key events and people of the period, the 34th President, Dwight David Eisenhower, dominated the 1950s as no other American public figure did.

"Ike," the soldier-citizen who gained the Republicans their first Presidency since Hoover, proved tremendously popular with the electorate. Whether this appeal was despite or because of his image as a nonintellectual who preferred honing his golf game to running the nation is unclear. What was clear, as **document 34**, The Gallup Poll, bears out, was that his public style found acceptance. Because of his engaging grin, low-key personality, and unpretentious manner, Eisenhower proved well insulated from the criticism attached to many of his administration's policies, especially those of his second term.

In spite of his popularity, he was not without detractors. His quiet demeanor, oratorical limitations, and reliance upon colorless careerists who joined the President in speaking "bureaucratese" sometimes led to gibes. Wags of the time referred to his administration as "the bland leading the bland"; and then-anonymous Oliver Jensen altered the Gettysburg Address to accommodate what he regarded as Eisenhower's characteristically cautious way of speaking. That version began:

> I haven't checked these figures, but 87 years ago, I think it was, a number of individuals organized a governmental setup here in this country, I believe it covered certain eastern areas, with this idea they were following up, based on a sort of national-independence arrangement and the program that every individual is as good as every other individual.

Eisenhower's centrist approach to politics did not always find favor within or without his party. Although he continued New Deal social programs, he was concerned enough about balancing the budget that large-scale federal expenditures often met his resistance. Since the Republicans controlled only the Senate in his first term and neither House of Congress in his second, bipartisan maneuvers by congressional leaders and Cabinet officers were necessary for the passage of significant legislation. **Document 35** is a photograph of some of the figures who played large roles during that period, including Charles Halleck, Allen Dulles, Everett Dirksen, Christian Herter, Sam Rayburn, Neil McElroy, Lyndon Johnson, and Richard Nixon.

One of the most courageous members of Congress was Senator Margaret Chase Smith of Maine (shown in **document 36**). In 1950, Senator Smith spoke out against the excesses of McCarthyism while others remained silent. In remarks made in a speech entitled a "Declaration of Conscience," she reminded all Americans that the Constitution itself provided for freedom of speech and the right to dissent, and that for practicing these freedoms one should not necessarily be labeled "Communist."

One man who shared her passion for civil liberties was the Reverend Martin Luther King, Jr. Dr. King, however, suggested civil disobedience could be a legitimate tactic for the civil rights movement if the government continued to sanction unequal political and societal status for black Americans (see **document 12**). He asserted, during a "Meet the Press" interview (**sound recording B**), that passive resistance to discriminatory local laws in fact supported constitutionally endowed civil rights.

Another religious figure, the Reverend Billy Graham, pictured in **document 37**, led and reflected a national resurgence of religious values. These values emerged when legislation included the phrase "under God" in the Pledge of Allegiance. Graham's style was much like Eisenhower's, for they shared several qualities, not the least being organizational ability, wide appeal to others, and faith in America.

However, there were signs of unrest with establishment values among America's younger generation. This was being expressed in a number of ways: vicarious identification with antihero movie stars James Dean and Marlon Brando, the fashionability of "beatnik" poetry, and the emergence of rock 'n' roll.

The biggest rock 'n' roll star of the 1950s was Elvis Presley. He embodied, for older Americans, something sinister, accelerating, and unfathomable; for their offspring, something exotic, daring, and forbidden. His induction into the army created a public furor among teenagers as represented in **document 38**, a March 1958 letter from three of these concerned fans. Ironically, Presley himself made no protest against serving and quietly did so.

Eisenhower was also popular with world leaders such as Charles de Gaulle of France and Nikita Khrushchev of the U.S.S.R., although their cordial personal relationships had limited practical diplomatic results. Despite amicable state visits, neither NATO ally de Gaulle **(document 39)** nor Cold War rival Khrushchev **(document 40)** acknowledged the validity of positions taken toward their countries by an often truculent Secretary of State John Foster Dulles.

Today many revisionist historians give Eisenhower higher marks as a statesman than he generally received at the time. They tend to view him as a sophisticated corporate manager who consulted and farmed out responsibilities while retaining authority, a coach who encouraged individuals on a team to work out problems in an atmosphere of cohesion and consensus, and a war hero who was capable of resisting war when it seemed most likely. In addition, an admirable sense of balance brought him to publicly warn in his farewell address, **sound recording E**, against a government run primarily by technocrats and what he called "the military-industrial complex," even though at various times during his tenure he had allowed scientific, military, and business interests to have considerable influence on federal policy. Thus, in the years since he left office, Eisenhower's stature has increased.

Time: 2 class periods

Objectives:

- To identify key events and people of the 1950s.

- To conduct research into dominant personalities of the 1950s.

- To analyze sound recordings to assess the effectiveness of the speakers.

Materials Needed:

Documents 33-40
Sound recordings B and E
Sound Recording Analysis worksheet, p. 15

Procedures:

1. Duplicate document 33 and distribute a copy to each student. Instruct the students to take the cartoon home and work with their parents to identify the images in the cartoon. Make a transparency of the cartoon, show it to the class, and color in the images as they are correctly identified.

    Note: you may instead use the cartoon as a pre- and post-test for a unit on the 1950s.

2. Distribute copies of documents 33-40 to the students. With the class, list on the chalkboard the names of personalities included in the documents. Assign a different personality to each student for research. Using material available in the documents, the school library and media center, and the local library and archives, ask students to gather information on the person and to represent the personality either in a descriptive paragraph, a drawing, a dialogue, or a cartoon. Post the results on the bulletin board along with the document facsimiles.

3. As a spelling exercise, ask the students to design a word puzzle using the names of as many of the personalities in this exercise as possible.

4. Duplicate the Sound Recording Analysis worksheet and distribute 2 copies to each student. Play sound recordings B and E and ask the students to complete a worksheet for each recording. Follow with a class discussion comparing the voice quality, accents, rhythm, pacing, confidence, and persuasiveness of Dr. King and President Eisenhower. (Include other samples of speeches made by these two personalities in this exercise if they are available.)

5. Extended activity: Ask the students to write an essay on President Eisenhower's personality based on evidence found in documents 33-40, 8, and 19, and sound recording E.

Cartoon Answers

1. Alaskan Statehood
2. Dwight D. Eisenhower
3. T.V. Westerns
4. *Explorer I*
5. Fidel Castro
6. Sir Edmund Hillary on Mt. Everest
7. Hawaiian Statehood
8. Volkswagen
9. Hungarian Revolution
10. Salk Polio Vaccination
11. Sea Hunt
12. Dwight D. Eisenhower
13. Finned Automobiles
14. Adlai Stevenson, Jr.
15. Gamal Abdel Nasser and the Suez Canal
16. Senator Joseph McCarthy
17. Queen Elizabeth II's Coronation
18. Dwight D. Eisenhower
19. Disneyland
20. Nikita Khrushchev's De-Stalinization Program
21. Richard M. Nixon
22. International Geophysical Year
23. African Revolutions
24. *Sputnik* and Satellites
25. Marilyn Monroe
26. Elvis Presley

Note: Alaska was the 49th state rather than the 50th (which was Hawaii), as the cartoon mistakenly labels it.

Exercise 9
Summary Exercise: Careers and History

Note to the Teacher:

In addition to the informational exercises suggested in the teachers guide, this collection of documents presents an opportunity to acquaint your students with potential areas of employment or interest in the field of history. Beyond education, there are a number of avenues to explore. The following examples may be implemented as special projects during the semester.

Time: Flexible

Objectives:

- To examine some aspects of applied history as a career or hobby.

- To demonstrate an understanding of the interrelationship of the documents as a group.

- To design and prepare a special interest project that demonstrates an application of the history and content of a group of documents.

Materials Needed:

Documents 1-40
Sound recordings A-E

Procedures:

Describe the following projects and ask the students to choose one to develop.

1. **Exhibition:** Design and construct an exhibition using the documents included in the packet. The plan should include a theme or a concept; consideration of exhibition methods, such as display, color, and design; definition of an audience for the exhibit; a script, including title, introductory materials, and captions; a schedule; and a layout.

2. **Appraisal of documents:** Archivists are required to determine what documents are retained as permanently valuable. Assume that each of the documents represents part of a collection of documents of that kind. Write an appraisal report detailing what documents you would keep, in part or entirely, and why. Consider the research value, legal value, and intrinsic value of the documents; i.e., the value the document may have because of its rarity, the signatures it bears, or its appearance. Make a list of what you need to know about the related topics of research and how these documents would help with that research. Consider what archivists must consider when appraising documents.

3. **Oral history:** Using the documents in the package, make a list of topics represented and a list of questions for an oral interview with several people who recall the 1950s. Interview a

representative sample of people who had varying experiences during the 1950s; for example, select people of various ages and races, a representative of each major political party, a military person, a mother of a soldier in Korea or early Vietnam. Review oral history fieldwork techniques from a good written source and design a plan. Emphasize the historical value of the interview. Use a tape recorder for the interviews, if possible. Produce a transcript from at least one interview, including the name, age, address, and a brief identification of the source; the place, time, and context of the interview; and the narrative. Consider the possible uses of these interviews; e.g., a series of published articles or a book, a radio or television program, etc.

Time Line

1953	**January 20**	Dwight D. Eisenhower is inaugurated as 34th President of the United States. Richard Nixon becomes Vice President.
	April 11	Department of Health, Education, and Welfare becomes operational with Mrs. Oveta Culp Hobby as first Secretary.
	June 8	Supreme Court rules that restaurants in the District of Columbia may not discriminate against black customers.
	June 19	Julius and Ethel Rosenberg are executed in Sing Sing Prison in New York.
	July 27	Armistice, ending the "police action" in Korea, goes into effect. Total U.S. casualties: 33,629 battle deaths, 20,617 deaths from other causes, 103,284 wounded.
	July 31	Robert A. Taft, Republican Senator from Ohio and powerful conservative force in the Senate, dies at age 63.
	September 8	Supreme Court Chief Justice Frederick M. Vinson dies at age 63 in Washington, DC.
	October 5	California Governor Earl Warren takes oath as the new Supreme Court Chief Justice. (Senate confirmation comes on March 1, 1954.)
	October 30	Gen. George C. Marshall is named the 1953 winner of the Nobel Prize for Peace for his work with the economic rebuilding of Europe after World War II.
1954	**January 21**	The U.S.S. *Nautilus*, the first atomic-powered submarine, is christened by Mrs. Dwight D. Eisenhower in Groton, CT.
	March 1	3 men and 1 woman, screaming "Freedom for Puerto Rico," open fire from the visitor's gallery on the floor of the House of Representatives. 5 Congressmen are wounded.
	April 8	President Eisenhower outlines concerns over the spread of communism in Southeast Asia and introduces his "domino theory."
	April 22-June 17	Army-McCarthy hearings take place in the U.S. Senate. Americans see McCarthy for the first time on national TV and dislike what they see. McCarthy's power begins to wane.
	May 7	Vietnamese forces led by Ho Chi Minh defeat French troops at the fortress of Dien Bien Phu, ending the French attempt to reestablish colonial domination of Vietnam.
	May 13	The St. Lawrence Seaway Development Act is signed. It calls for cooperation between the United States and Canada to open the Great Lakes to oceangoing ships.
	May 17	The Supreme Court rules that segregated schools are illegal in the landmark case of *Brown v. The Board of Education of Topek*a.
	June 29	CIA-sponsored coup overthrows elected government in Guatemala.
	July 17	First jazz festival is held in Newport, RI. The Newport Jazz Festival would become a showcase for the best of that kind of music.
	July 20	The United States joins France, Great Britain, China, the U.S.S.R., Laos, and Communist and non-Communist governments of Vietnam in the Geneva Accords. The United States eventually refuses to sign the agreement but vows to do nothing to "disturb" the process of peace in Vietnam.
	November 28	Physicist Enrico Fermi, one of the developers of the atomic bomb, dies at age 53.
	December 2	The U.S. Senate votes 67 to 22 to censure Wisconsin Senator Joseph McCarthy for conduct "that tends to bring the Senate into dishonor and disrepute...."

1955	January 28	Congress passes a resolution giving President Eisenhower permission to use U.S. forces to defend the Formosa Straits from Communist attack.
	April 12	After extensive testing, Dr. Jonas Salk's vaccine for prevention of poliomyelitis is declared safe and effective and a program is started to vaccinate all the children in the United States.
	April 18	Scientist Albert Einstein, best known for his theory of relativity, dies in New Jersey at age 76.
	August 12	Eisenhower signs a measure raising the federal minimum wage from 75 cents to $1 an hour.
	September 30	James Dean, the young heartthrob method actor, star of *Rebel Without a Cause* and *East of Eden*, dies in an automobile accident in California at age 24.
	November 1	Dale Carnegie, author of *How to Win Friends and Influence People*, dies in New York at age 66.
	November 25	The Interstate Commerce Commission outlaws segregation on interstate buses and trains.
	December 1	Rosa Parks, a black seamstress and part-time worker for the NAACP, is arrested in Montgomery, AL, for refusing to relinquish her seat on a bus to a white passenger. This sets in motion the Montgomery bus boycott and brings the young pastor of a local Baptist church, the Reverend Martin Luther King, Jr., into the national civil rights spotlight.
	December 5	The American Federation of Labor and the Congress of Industrial Organizations vote to merge into a single union, the AFL/CIO, and elect George Meany as the first president.
1956	March 12	101 Congressmen issue the "Declaration of Constitutional Principles," calling on states to resist the Supreme Court desegregation orders.
	April 21	10-year-old Leonard Ross wins $100,000 on a popular TV quiz show, to the amazement of the viewing audience.
	June 29	The Federal Aid Highway Act authorizes a 13-year program for 41,000 miles of state and interstate highways.
	July 25	The Italian ocean liner *Andrea Doria* is struck by the Swedish freighter *Stockholm*. The *Andrea Doria* sinks killing 50 people; 1,650 people are rescued.
	July 26	Egyptian leader Gamal Abdel Nasser nationalizes the Suez Canal.
	August 11	Jackson Pollock, the founder of the abstract expressionist school of art, dies in an automobile accident near East Hampton, NY.
	August 13-17	The Democratic Party nominates Adlai Stevenson for President, for the second time, and Tennessee Senator Estes Kefauver for Vice President at the party convention in Chicago.
	August 20-23	The Republican Party meets in San Francisco to renominate Eisenhower and Nixon.
	October 8	New York Yankee pitcher Don Larsen pitches the only no-hitter in World Series history. It is also a perfect game, the first in baseball since 1922.
	November 6	Eisenhower and Nixon are reelected when they defeat Stevenson and Kefauver by more than 9 million votes.
	December 13	The Supreme Court invalidates the Alabama law segregating public transportation.
1957	January 5	President Eisenhower asks Congress for permission to use U.S. forces to resist Communist aggression in the Middle East. Policy becomes known as the Eisenhower Doctrine.

January 14	Actor Humphrey Bogart, star of *Casablanca*, *The African Queen*, and *The Caine Mutiny*, dies in Hollywood, CA, at age 57.
March 11	Adm. Richard E. Byrd, the first man to fly over the North Pole, dies in Boston, MA, at age 68.
May 2	Senator Joseph McCarthy, the controversial Communist hunter, dies in Bethesda, MD, at age 47.
July 1	The International Geophysical Year begins. IGY was an 18-month study of the Earth by 10,000 scientists from 70 countries.
July 6	Althea Gibson wins the Wimbledon women's singles title, becoming the first black to win the women's tennis title.
September 4-25	The integration plan worked out in compliance with the Supreme Court rulings is thwarted by Arkansas Governor Orval Faubus. Eisenhower decides to federalize the National Guard and send the 101st Airborne Division to Little Rock to ensure the safety of the children.
October 4	The Soviet Union places an artificial satellite weighing 184 pounds into Earth orbit. This satellite, named *Sputnik 1*, astonished the U.S. public and led to greater emphasis on the teaching of scientific and technical studies in schools.
November 25	Eisenhower suffers a mild stroke.
December 6	U.S. rocket carrying a grapefruit-size satellite explodes upon launch at Cape Canaveral, FL.
December 6	AFL-CIO expels the Teamsters Union from their organization for corruption. Teamster leader Dave Beck is convicted of embezzlement, and Jimmy Hoffa is also suspected of wrongdoing.
December 18	First atomic power plant begins production of electricity in Shippingport, PA.

1958	January 31	The United States launches *Explorer 1*, its first successful artificial Earth satellite. It weighs 18 pounds and identifies the existence of the Van Allen radiation belt.
	June 28	The Mackinac Bridge, the second longest suspension bridge in the world, connecting the upper and lower peninsulas of Michigan, opens.
	July 15	Responding to a request from the Lebanese government, President Eisenhower sends U.S. Marines into Lebanon.
	July 29	The National Aeronautics and Space Administration (NASA) is established to provide civilian control of space exploration.
	August 5	The U.S.S. *Nautilus*, the first nuclear-powered submarine, surfaces near Spitsbergen after completing the first transpolar voyage beneath the arctic icepack. The trip takes 96 hours.
	October 4	The first scheduled jetliner service across the Atlantic begins. The British *Comet IV* makes the trip in 6 hours and 12 minutes.
	November 28	The United States successfully tests an intercontinental ballistic missile (ICBM).

1959	January 3	Alaska joins the union as the 49th state.
	January 7	The United States officially recognizes the revolutionary government of Manuel Urrutia in Cuba after the overthrow of the government of Fulgencio Batista. Urrutia's armed forces are led by Fidel Castro.
	April 9	Frank Lloyd Wright, architect, dies in his home in Phoenix, AZ, at age 89.
	May 24	John Foster Dulles, author of the aggressive foreign policy of the United States referred to as "brinksmanship," dies in Washington, DC, of cancer at age 71.
	June 11	Postmaster General Arthur E. Summerfield bans D.H. Lawrence's novel *Lady Chatterly's Lover* from the mail. The courts later overturn the ban.

June 26	Ingemar Johanson of Sweden wins the heavyweight boxing title by knocking out Floyd Patterson in New York.
July 23-August 2	Vice President Nixon visits the Soviet Union.
August 21	Hawaii joins the union as the 50th state.
September 15-27	Nikita Khrushchev visits the United States and meets with Eisenhower at Camp David, MD.

1960	February 2	Sit-ins begin at Woolworth's lunch counter in Greensboro, N.C.
	May 1-17	The downing over the Soviet Union of an American U-2 spy plane and the capture of its pilot, Francis Gary Powers, ends the thaw in the Cold War.
	May 6	The Civil Rights Act passes, enabling federal judges to order supervision of elections.
	May 16	Khrushchev lashes out at Eisenhower and scuttles the Paris summit.
	October 6-10	A special House subcommittee holds investigative hearings about TV quiz shows and finds instances of fixing.
	October 7-26	Presidential hopefuls John F. Kennedy and Richard Nixon engage in the first televised presidential campaign debates.
	October 20	Most exports to Cuba are embargoed by the United States.
	November 8	John F. Kennedy is elected President of the United States by the narrowest popular margin since 1884, approximately 113,000 votes.
		The technique of kidney dialysis is first used for medical therapy.
		"Fiorello!" wins the Pulitzer Prize.
		The first U.S. weather satellite orbits the Earth.

| 1961 | January 3 | Eisenhower breaks off diplomatic relations with Cuba. |
| | January 20 | John F. Kennedy is inaugurated the 35th President of the United States. Lyndon Johnson becomes Vice President. |

THE BETTER
YOU KNOW
AMERICA...
THE BETTER
THE FUTURE
LOOKS

Annotated Bibliography

Adams, John G. *Without Precedent: The Story of the Death of McCarthyism.* New York: W.W. Norton & Co., 1983.

> A personal account of the McCarthy investigations by a counsel to the army during the proceedings.

Altschull, J. Herbert. "Khrushchev and 'The Berlin Ultimatum': The Jackal Syndrome and the Cold War." *Journalism Quarterly* 54 (No. 3, 1977): 545-551, 565.

> An article posing several interpretations of the 1958 Khrushchev letter protesting the western occupation of Berlin.

Ambrose, Stephen E. *Eisenhower.* Vol. 2, *The President.* Norwalk, CT: Easton Press, 1987.

> An authoritative biography of Eisenhower during his White House years. Based on primary sources from the Dwight D. Eisenhower Presidential Library and written as a chronological narrative.

Barber, Noel. *Seven Days of Freedom, the Hungarian Uprising, 1956.* New York: Stein and Day Publishers, 1974.

> A personal account of the Hungarian revolution supported by interviews with major participants and examination of United Nations documents.

Bates, Daisy. *The Long Shadow of Little Rock – A Memoir.* Fayetteville: University of Arkansas Press, 1987.

> Ms. Bates, a black Little Rock, AR, journalist and also the NAACP's state president, considers the events surrounding the desegregation of Central High School, and how it affected the community.

Bernhard, Nancy E. *U.S. Television News and Cold War Propaganda, 1947-1960.* New York: Cambridge University Press, 1999.

> An intriguing look at the simultaneous course of the cold war and the rise of television, this work examines the extent to which the major news organizations cooperated with the U.S. government to censor the news most Americans received in the 1950s.

Blaustein, Albert P., and Zangrando, Robert L., eds. *Civil Rights and the American Negro, A Documentary History.* Evanston, IL: Northwestern University Press, 1991.

> The editors have brought together historical documents to record the struggle of blacks to secure civil rights throughout U.S. history, including the attempted desegregation of the armed forces, public housing, and public schools.

Bodron, Margaret M. "United States Intervention in Lebanon—1958." *Military Review* 56 (Feb. 1976): 66-76.

> The author explores the reasons behind the landing of U.S. troops in Lebanon by the Eisenhower administration during that country's 1958 civil war.

Bourne, Peter G. *Fidel: A Biography of Fidel Castro.* New York: Dodd, Mead & Co., 1986.

> A chronological account of Castro's life from childhood to the present. The author explores Castro's relationships with Celia Sanchez, Che Guevara, Nikita Khrushchev and other Soviet leaders, and U.S. Presidents. He uses information obtained from interviews and source documents to discuss Castro's reactions to the Bay of Pigs invasion, the Cuban Missile Crisis, and assassination attempts on his life.

Branch, Taylor. *Parting the Waters: America in the King Years, 1954-1963.* New York: Simon and Schuster, 1988.

> A comprehensive book of the early civil rights movement in the United States, this work looks at both the key figures in the movement and the broader experience for ordinary African Americans. This book has become essential background reading for any scholarship on the civil rights movement. The second volume in this series, *Pillar of Fire: America in the King Years, 1963-65,* covers the movement at the height of its influence.

Brendon, Piers. *Ike, His Life and Times.* New York: Harper & Row, 1986.

> Using sources at the Eisenhower Library to track Ike's military career and Presidential campaigns and tenure, the author explores Eisenhower's decision making processes and reactions to major events of his Presidency, including McCarthyism, Little Rock, and the U-2 incident.

Daniel, Pete. *Lost Revolutions: The South in the 1950s.* Chapel Hill: University of North Carolina Press for Smithsonian National Museum of American History, 2000.

> This work traces the myriad of changes that occurred in the South following World War II, from popular culture and agriculture to religion and politics. At the heart of many of these changes was increasing racial tension that led to the birth of the civil rights movement.

Dick, James C. "The Strategic Arms Race, 1957-1961: Who Opened a Missile Gap?" *Journal of Politics* 34 (No. 4, 1972): 1062-1110.

> The author theorizes that the supposed 1960 "Missile Gap" was primarily a political tactic used by the Democratic Party to enhance its chances for capturing the White House.

Divine, Robert A. *The Sputnik Challenge.* New York: Oxford University Press, 1993.

> Focusing on one episode in the space race between the United States and the Soviet Union, this book examines the shock and horror with which Americans learned that the Russians had managed to launch a satellite that orbited the Earth before them. The work illustrates the far-reaching impact on American culture and society, as Americans came to fear that the Soviets had become more advanced in all sorts of respects.

Doyle, Edward; Lipsman, Samuel; and Weiss, Stephen. *Passing the Torch.* Boston: Boston Publishing Company, 1981.

> Part of an overall series, *The Vietnam Experience,* this volume traces the history of Vietnam following World War II, when the United States' relationship with France led the former into involvement in the North-South Vietnamese conflict.

Eisenhower, Dwight D. *Mandate for Change, The White House Years.* v2. Garden City: Doubleday & Company, 1963-65.

> In his autobiography, Eisenhower describes reasons for accepting the Republican nomination for President and his subsequent actions as President. Includes information on the foreign and domestic policies of his first term.

Ferrell, Robert H., ed. *The Eisenhower Diaries.* New York: Norton, 1981.

> From 1935 to his retirement on January 20, 1961, Eisenhower kept a diary revealing his thoughts about major actions and events that affected him. Includes his reasoning for many of the significant decisions made during his administration.

Finer, Herman. *Dulles Over Suez, The Theory and Practice of His Diplomacy.* Chicago: Quadrangle Books, 1964.

> A diplomatic history involving decisions made by John Foster Dulles during the Suez Crisis of 1956. Most relevant official documents were still security-classified when this book was being published, forcing the author to rely heavily upon interviews with significant role players.

Gettleman, Marvin E., et al. *Vietnam and America, A Documented History.* 2d ed. New York: Grove Press, 1995.

> A history of Vietnam with emphasis on the U.S. involvement after World War II through the fall of Saigon in 1975. Utilizes government-generated primary sources.

Greenstein, Fred I., *The Hidden-hand Presidency: Eisenhower as Leader.* New York: Basic Books, 1982.

> A critical reevaluation of the presidential style of Dwight D. Eisenhower, this work dispels the notion that Ike was not involved in the running of the government and allowed his advisors to operate with almost complete autonomy. Rather, Greenstein presents a picture of the president as a diplomatic and careful manipulator, who played a much larger role in domestic and foreign affairs than previously thought.

Hand, Jeffrey. *When The Going Was Good!* New York: Crown Publishers, 1982.

> A provocative social history of the 1950s treating topics as diverse as McCarthyism, rock 'n' roll, theology, and sports.

Hoopes, Townsend. *The Devil and John Foster Dulles.* Boston: Little, Brown, and Company, 1973.

> In this biographical narrative, the author examines the rigidity of Dulles' policies and actions as Secretary of State, particularly those of an anti-Communist nature.

Hoyt, Edwin P. *The Bloody Road to Panmunjom.* New York: Stein & Day, 1985.

> A critical look at the Korean war, with emphasis on the role of the U.S. military — particularly its inability to gather and analyze vital intelligence information and its rejection of information offered by other member nations of the United Nations.

Immerman, Richard H. *The CIA in Guatemala: The Foreign Policy of Intervention.* Austin: University of Texas Press, 1982.

> An authoritative history of CIA covert activities and the 1954 coup d'etat in Guatemala. Sees U.S. foreign policy toward Guatemala as less concerned with bilateral relations than with containment of communism.

_____. *John Foster Dulles and the Diplomacy of the Cold War.* Princeton, NJ: Princeton University Press, 1990.

> A collection of nine essays, this work paints a complex portrait of Secretary of State Dulles during the height of the cold war, showing how Dulles left an enduring imprint on American foreign policy.

Jenkins, Roy. "Adlai Stevenson." *American Heritage* 24 (October 1973): 20-23, 96-100.

> A brief biography of Stevenson, focusing on his political career and his role in the Democratic Party.

Joy, Charles Turner. *Negotiating While Fighting: The Diary of Admiral C. Turner Joy at the Korean Armistice Conference.* Edited by Allan E. Goodman. Stanford: Hoover Institution Press, 1978.

> A discussion of that armistice by the senior U.S. delegate. The author identifies key participants, chronicles the progress of the talks, and offers his view of the promises and pitfalls contained within the negotiation process itself.

Karnow, Stanley. *Vietnam, A History.* 2d rev. ed. New York: Penguin Books, 1997.

> An authoritative history of U.S. involvement in Vietnam from the death of the first U.S. soldier to the fall of Saigon, April 30, 1975. Relies upon government documents and interviews with officials on both sides of the conflict as sources. This book is the companion text to the PBS television series, "Vietnam: a Television History."

Kennan, George F. *Memoirs, 1950-1963*. Vol. 2. Boston: Little, Brown, and Company, 1972.

> Kennan, a career diplomat, wielded great influence on U.S. foreign policy due to his expertise in U.S. and Soviet relations. His memoirs contain a copy of Foreign Service Dispatch No. 116, dated September 8, 1952, which essentially laid out the U.S. policy of containment.

_____. *Russia, The Atom and the West*. Westport, CT: Greenwood Press, 1974.

> A collection of Kennan's Reith Lectures delivered over the BBC in Great Britain and CBS in the United States addressing such topics as the psychology of the Soviets and its effect on their foreign policy; the military aspect of the U.S./U.S.S.R. power struggle; the status of the U.S.S.R.; and the U.S.S.R.'s progress in industry.

Killian, James R., Jr. *Sputnik, Scientists and Eisenhower*. Cambridge: MIT Press, 1977.

> Eisenhower's science adviser describes the relationship that developed between science and the Presidency after the Soviet launching of Sputnik.

King, Martin Luther, Jr. *Stride Toward Freedom, The Montgomery Story*. New York: Harper and Brothers, 1958.

> A personal narrative describing the mood of the Montgomery, AL, black community before and during its boycott of public transportation. The volume traces the development of the strategy of nonviolent civil disobedience by the community and its leaders. It follows their challenge of the segregation laws to the Supreme Court.

Lewis, David L. *King, A Biography*. 2d ed. Chicago: University of Illinois Press, 1978.

> A historical biography of the civil rights activist Martin Luther King, Jr. It examines the evolution of his philosophy from his family's activism in civil rights as a youth through his university years and beyond. In the second edition, the author includes information concerning King's assassination and the FBI's surveillance of King.

Marchetti, Victor, and Marks, John D. *The CIA and the Cult of Intelligence*. New York: Alfred A. Knopf, 1974.

> The author was a mid-level CIA employee who was dissatisfied with the shift of agency focus from the ". . . overall supervision, coordination and processing of intelligence" to covert operations. The goal of the book was to initiate reforms in the CIA. Many passages in the text were deleted by CIA censorship. Some of the topics discussed include CIA involvement in Guatemala, Iran, the Cuban Missile Crisis, Tibetan Revolt, Bay of Pigs, the Congo, Vietnam, and the 1970 Chilean elections.

Mauldin, Bill. *What's Got Your Back Up?* New York: Harper and Brothers, 1961.

> The book contains political cartoons from 1958 through 1961 by the prizewinning cartoonist. Subjects covered include civil rights, union leaders, Khrushchev, Mao and China, de Gaulle and Algeria, U.S. domestic policies, the Middle East, Castro and Cuba, and the television quiz-show scandal.

Miller, Douglas T., and Nowak, Marion. *The Fifties: The Way We Really Were*. Garden City: Doubleday, 1977.

> A comprehensive social history, with some political history, that contrasts the events of the 1950s with the mood of the era.

Neff, Donald. *Warriors at Suez*. New York: Linden Press/Simon and Schuster, 1981.

> This book follows the courses taken by the U.S.S.R., Great Britain, France, Israel, Egypt, and the United States during the 1956 Suez Crisis. The author describes the motivations for collusion between Great Britain, France, and Israel in their joint invasion of Egypt and the entrance of the United States into the Middle East as mediator.

Oshinsky, David M. *A Conspiracy So Immense: The World of Joe McCarthy.* New York: Free Press, 1983.

A well-crafted account of the life of Joseph McCarthy and the history of McCarthyism, this work captures the complex nature of McCarthy's ambiguous personality. Oshinsky is determined to explain, but does not excuse, McCarthy's leadership of the red scare of the 1950s.

Rhodes, Richard. " 'I am Become Death . . .' The Agony of J. Robert Oppenheimer." *American Heritage* 28 (Oct. 1977):70-83.

A brief biography of world-famous atomic physicist Julius Robert Oppenheimer. The author follows Oppenheimer's educational and philosophical development, his contributions to physics, and the events surrounding the loss of his security clearance.

Roosevelt, Kermit. *Countercoup, The Struggle for Control of Iran.* New York: McGraw-Hill, 1979.

A personal account of the U.S. involvement in the overthrow of Mossadegh and the reinstallation of the Shah in Iran by the mastermind of the operation. The author describes the plans of the operation step by step.

Schlesinger, Stephen, and Kinzer, Stephen. *Bitter Fruit: The Story of the American Coup in Guatemala.* exp. ed. Boston: Harvard University, David Rockefeller Center for Latin American Studies, 1999.

A political history of U.S. involvement in the 1954 overthrow of the Arbenz regime in Guatemala. The book explores the question of whether Arbenz was a threat to the United States or just to the United Fruit Company.

Schrecker, Ellen. *Many Are the Crimes: McCarthyism in America.* Boston: Little, Brown, 1998.

A history of communism and anticommunism in modern American history, this work spans the 1930s to early 1990s. It discusses the key leaders and ideas of the American communist movement, the way American communists attempted to disseminate their political philosophy across the United States, and the various forms of political repression with which these efforts were met.

Sinclair, Andrew. *Che Guevara.* New York: Sutton Pub. Ltd., 1998.

A biography of Ernesto Guevara that describes the events in his life that led to the development of his radical political philosophy. The book recounts his experiences as a guerilla fighter in the mountains of Cuba.

Stavins, Ralph; Garnet, Richard J.; and Raskin, Marcus G. *Washington Plans an Aggressive War, A Documented Account of the United States Adventure in Indochina.* New York: Random House, 1971.

The authors made use of interviews, government documents, and the "Pentagon Papers" as sources for their book. They acknowledge their biases against the war. The book focuses on the planning stages of U.S. involvement in Vietnam, the motivation and mentality of the officials involved, the implementation process, and the role of the bureaucracy.

York, Herbert F. "Eisenhower's Other Warning." *Physics Today* 30 (Jan. 1977): 9-11.

This article focuses on Eisenhower's farewell address and its less-noted warning against the power the scientific elite may have or may develop and exert on governmental policy.

Peace and Prosperity: 1953-1961
Archival Citations of Documents

1. Photograph of President Eisenhower and Mamie Eisenhower watching Richard Nixon's "Checkers speech" on television, September 23, 1952; Folder 17; Box 48-3; Dwight D. Eisenhower Library, Abilene, KS.

2. Photograph No. 62-187; "President Eisenhower, Roy Rogers, Dale Evans, and others attending grandson David Eisenhower's birthday party," March 31, 1956; Dwight D. Eisenhower Library, Abilene, KS.

3. Photograph No. 72-1774-3; "President Eisenhower with Jane Powell, Bob Hope, Pearl Bailey, and others," June 7, 1956; Dwight D. Eisenhower Library, Abilene, KS.

4. Photograph No. 72-176-1; "President Eisenhower throwing out the first ball for the opening game of the 1956 World Series," October 3, 1956; Dwight D. Eisenhower Library, Abilene, KS.

5. "The Future of America," booklet released by the Advertising Council, 1954; File of the Special Assistant; Civil Defense General-54; Box 12; Office of Coordinating Government Public Service Announcements; Dwight D. Eisenhower Library, Abilene, KS.

6. Photograph No. 306-NT-316H-1; "Senator Joseph R. McCarthy," March 14, 1950; Records of the U.S. Information Agency, Record Group 306; National Archives at College Park, College Park, MD.

7. Enabling decision in *Brown v. Board of Education of Topeka, Kansas*, May 31, 1955; Case 1, O.T. 1954; Appellate Jurisdiction Case Files, 1792-;Records of the Supreme Court of the United States, Record Group 267; National Archives Building, Washington, DC.

8. Text released to the press regarding the Little Rock crisis, September 24, 1957;Whitman speech series; Integration-Little Rock, AR; Box 22; Dwight D. Eisenhower Library, Abilene, KS.

9. House Resolution 6127, which established the Civil Rights Commission, April 1, 1957; Bill Files of the Judiciary Committee (HR 85-A-DIO); 85th Congress, 1st Session; Records of the U.S. House of Representatives, Record Group 233; National Archives Building, Washington, DC.

10. House Report 291 from the Judiciary Committee, reporting favorably on H. R. 6127, April 1, 1957; Bill Files of the Judiciary Committee (HR85-ADIO); 85th Congress, 1st Session; Records of the U.S. House of Representatives, Record Group 233; National Archives Building, Washington, DC.

11. Memorandum by E. Frederic Morrow on the student protest movement in the South, March 7, 1960; XOF 142-A-4; Box 731-1; Central Files; Official Files; Dwight D. Eisenhower Library, Abilene, KS.

12. Resolution of the United Postal Workers' Association (UPWA) urging President Eisenhower to conduct a civil rights fact-finding tour of the South, April 6, 1957; 142-A - "Negro Matters, Colored Question"; Box 731-1; Central Files, Official Files; Dwight D. Eisenhower Library, Abilene, KS.

13. Photograph No. 65-451; "President Eisenhower with Doctor Jonas Salk, inventor of the polio vaccine," April 22, 1955; Dwight D. Eisenhower Library, Abilene, KS.

14. Memo from Don Cadle, head of OMB's Military Division to the Director of OMB comparing U. S. and Soviet space programs, March 2, 1960; File P8-1; BOB Series 52.1; Records of the Office of Management and Budget, Record Group 51; National Archives at College Park, College Park, MD.

15. "How Could You Know Tonight was the Night?," Civil Defense poster, 1954; Civil Defense General, 1954; Box 12; File of Special Assistant, Office of Coordinating Government Public Service Announcements; Dwight D. Eisenhower Library, Abilene, KS.

16. Message from Commander, Air Technical Information Center to Commander, Air Defense Command reporting the sighting of an unidentified flying object with sketch of location, December 3, 1957; Project Bluebook # 5415; Records of Headquarters U.S. Air Force, Record Group 341; National Archives at College Park, College Park, MD.

17. Photograph No. 72-2753-2; "President Eisenhower with young pianist Van Cliburn," May 23, 1958; Dwight D. Eisenhower Library, Abilene, KS.

18. Translation of letter from Soviet Premier Nikita Khrushchev to President Eisenhower upon the visit of Vice President Nixon to the Soviet Union, August 1959; Folder: Vice President's trip to Russia; Box 7; White House Office; Office of the Staff Secretary; Dwight D. Eisenhower Library, Abilene, KS.

19. Memo outlining U. S. objectives and tactics for conversation for the visit of Premier Khrushchev to the United States, September 11, 1959; Folder: Vice President's trip to Russia; Box 7; White House Office, Office of the Staff Secretary; Dwight D. Eisenhower Library, Abilene, KS.

20. Photograph No. 79-5-8; "The Moscow exhibit of Francis Gary Powers and his U-2 reconnaissance aircraft," May 1960; Morgan, Gerald D; Box 79-5; Dwight D. Eisenhower Library, Abilene, KS.

21. Special staff note containing information from the United States Information Agency on their handling of the failure of the Paris summit, May 19, 1960; Toner Notes, May 1960; Box 49; Eisenhower, D. D., Papers of the Presidential Diary; Dwight D. Eisenhower Library, Abilene, KS.

22. Statement by President Eisenhower upon the signing of the Korean Armistice, July 26, 1953; Ann Whitman Files; Korean 1953 (1); Box 32; Eisenhower Papers; Dwight D. Eisenhower Library, Abilene, KS.

23. Letter from Mrs. Barnard Cummings to President Eisenhower regarding her son's being held as a prisoner of war in North Korea, September 6, 1953; Official Prisoners of War; OF 154-H (1); Box 822; Central Files; Dwight D. Eisenhower Library, Abilene, KS.

24. Mutual Defense Treaty between the United States and the Republic of Korea, October 1, 1953; 383.21, Korea, Section 132; Geographic File, Korea, 1951-1953; Records of the U.S. Joint Chiefs of Staff, Record Group 218; National Archives at College Park, College Park, MD.

25. Point paper, "A Concept for Action with Regard to Indochina," May 13, 1954; 091-Indochina, May-June 1954; Chairman's File, Admiral Radford, 1953-1957; Records of the U. S. Joint Chiefs of Staff, Record Group 218; National Archives at College Park, College Park, MD.

26. Letter from Vietnamese Premier Diem to President Eisenhower on the occasion of the fifth anniversary of the Republic of Vietnam, November 8, 1960; International Series; Vietnam (1); Box 50; Eisenhower Papers; Dwight D. Eisenhower Library, Abilene, KS.

27. Memorandum to Admiral Felix Stump, Commander in Chief Pacific Fleet, regarding the evacuation of refugees from Haiphong to Saigon, August 30, 1954; 091-Indochina, August 1954; Chairman's File, Admiral Radford; Records of the U. S. Joint Chiefs of Staff, Record Group 218; National Archives at College Park, College Park, MD.

28. Memorandum from Gerard Smith to Gordon Gray regarding the political situation in Iran, September 5, 1958; Iran Political (57-60); Box 11; Office of the Special Assistant to the National Security Advisor; White House Office; Dwight D. Eisenhower Library, Abilene, KS.

29. Translation of telegram from Guatemalan President Miguel Fuentes to President Eisenhower thanking him for supporting his government against communist guerillas, November 19, 1960; International; Guatemala (1); Box 24; Eisenhower, D. D., Papers of the President; Dwight D. Eisenhower Library, Abilene, KS.

30. Advertisement for Radio Free Europe, 1954; "Crusade for Freedom Campaigns;" Files of the Special Assistant, Office of Coordinating Government Public Service Announcements; Box 12; Dwight D. Eisenhower Library, Abilene, KS.

31. Photograph No. 56-22137; "Hungarian freedom fighters riding on a captured Soviet T-55 tank," Budapest, October 1956; Demonstrations, Hungary, Records of the U.S. Information Agency, Record Group 306; National Archives at College, College Park, MD.

32. Map of the Suez Canal, July 30, 1941; Army Map Service P572, 1:250,000 Suez Canal; Records of the Office of the Chief of Engineers, Record Group 77; National Archives at College Park, College Park, MD.

33. Cartoon, "Images of the Fifties," January 1961; *Deseret News*; NAF 8994; Dwight D. Eisenhower Library, Abilene, KS.

34. Washington Post, Gallup Poll related to President Eisenhower's popularity, August 7, 1955; OF 142-A04(1); Central Files Official Files; Box 731-1; Dwight D. Eisenhower Library, Abilene, KS.

35. Photograph No. 72-3004-2; "President Eisenhower, Vice President Nixon, and congressional leaders, including Senator Lyndon Johnson," March 6, 1959; Dwight D. Eisenhower Library, Abilene, KS.

36. Photograph No. 306-50-2746; "Senator Margaret Chase Smith," n.d.; Records of the U.S. Information Agency, Record Group 306; National Archives at College Park, College Park, MD.

37. Photograph No. 67-693; "Dwight D. Eisenhower with Billy Graham," August 8, 1952; Dwight D. Eisenhower Library, Abilene, KS.

38. Letter from fans of Elvis Presley to President Eisenhower regarding cutting his hair after induction in the Army, March 1958; NAF 8863; Dwight D. Eisenhower Library, Abilene, KS.

39. Translation of letter from French president Charles de Gaulle to President Eisenhower, May 20, 1960; De Gaulle; International Series, Box 12; DDE-Papers as Pres.; Dwight D. Eisenhower Library, Abilene, KS.

40. Photograph No. 73-757-15; "President Eisenhower with Soviet premier Nikita Khrushchev," September 25, 1959; Dwight D. Eisenhower Library, Abilene, KS.

41. Sound Recording 200-709 #3; "The Army/McCarthy hearings including the words of Army chief counsel Joseph Welch, counsel Roy Cohn, and Senator Joseph McCarthy, narration by Fred Fisher," June 9, 1954; National Archives Collections of Donated Materials; National Archives at College Park, College Park, MD.

42. Sound Recording 200.2201; "Reverend Martin Luther King on the NBC program 'Meet the Press,'" 1960; National Archives Collection of Donated Materials; National Archives at College Park, College Park, MD.

43. Sound Recording 200-388; "An atomic weapon test at Yucca Flats, Nevada, by reporter Charles Collingwood," March 17, 1953; National Archives Collection of Donated Materials; National Archives at College Park, College Park, MD.

44. Sound Recording 200.1688; "The 'Kitchen Debate' between Soviet premier Nikita Khrushchev and Vice President Richard Nixon in Moscow," July 24, 1959; National Archives Collection of Donated Materials; National Archives at College Park, College Park, MD.

45. Sound Recording 200.201.593; "President Eisenhower's farewell address," January 17, 1961; National Archives Collection of Donated Materials; National Archives at College Park, College Park, MD.

About the National Archives:
A Word to Educators

The National Archives and Records Administration (NARA) is responsible for the preservation and use of the permanently valuable records of the federal government. These materials provide evidence of the activities of the government from 1774 to the present in the form of written and printed documents, maps and posters, sound recordings, photographs, films, computer tapes, and other media. These rich archival sources are useful to everyone: federal officials seeking information on past government activities, citizens needing data for use in legal matters, historians, social scientists and public policy planners, environmentalists, historic preservationists, medical researchers, architects and engineers, novelists and playwrights, journalists researching stories, students preparing papers, and persons tracing their ancestry or satisfying their curiosity about particular historical events. These records are useful to you as educators either in preparing your own instructional materials or pursuing your own research.

The National Archives records are organized by the governmental body that created them rather than under a library's subject/author/title categories. There is no Dewey decimal or Library of Congress designation; each departmental bureau or collection of agency's records is assigned a record group number. In lieu of a card catalog, inventories and other finding aids assist the researcher in locating material in records not originally created for research purposes, often consisting of thousands of cubic feet of documentation.

The National Archives is a public institution whose records and research facilities nationwide are open to anyone 14 years of age and over. These facilities are found in the Washington, DC, metropolitan area, in the 11 Presidential libraries, the Nixon Presidential Materials Project, and in 16 regional archives across the nation. Whether you are pursuing broad historical questions or are interested in the history of your family, admittance to the research room at each location requires only that you fill out a simple form stating your name, address, and research interest. A staff member then issues an identification card, which is good for two years.

If you come to do research, you will be offered an initial interview with a reference archivist. You will also be able to talk with archivists who have custody of the records. If you have a clear definition of your questions and have prepared in advance by reading as many of the secondary sources as possible, you will find that these interviews can be very helpful in guiding you to the research material you need.

The best printed source of information about the overall holdings of the National Archives is the *Guide to the National Archives of the United States* (issued in 1974, reprinted in 1988), which is available in university libraries and many public libraries and online at **www.nara.gov**. The *Guide* describes in very general terms the records in the National Archives, gives the background and history of each agency represented by those records, and provides useful information about access to the records. To accommodate users outside of Washington, DC, the regional archives hold microfilm copies of much that is found in Washington. In addition, the regional archives contain records created by field offices of the federal government, including district and federal appellate court records, records of the Bureau of Indian Affairs, National Park Service, Bureau of Land Management, Forest Service, Bureau of the Census, and others. These records are particularly useful for local and regional history studies and in linking local with national historical events.

For more information about the National Archives and its educational and cultural programs, visit NARA's Web site at **www.nara.gov**.

Presidential Libraries

Herbert Hoover Library
210 Parkside Drive
West Branch, IA 52358-0488
319-643-5301

Franklin D. Roosevelt Library
511 Albany Post Road
Hyde Park, NY 12538-1999
914-229-8114

Harry S. Truman Library
500 West U.S. Highway 24
Independence, MO 64050-1798
816-833-1400

Dwight D. Eisenhower Library
200 Southeast Fourth Street
Abilene, KS 67410-2900
785-263-4751

John Fitzgerald Kennedy Library
Columbia Point
Boston, MA 02125-3398
617-929-4500

Lyndon Baines Johnson Library
2313 Red River Street
Austin, TX 78705-5702
512-916-5137

Gerald R. Ford Library
1000 Beal Avenue
Ann Arbor, MI 48109-2114
734-741-2218

Jimmy Carter Library
441 Freedom Parkway
Atlanta, GA 30307-1498
404-331-3942

Ronald Reagan Library
40 Presidential Drive
Simi Valley, CA 93065-0600
805-522-8444/800-410-8354

George Bush Library
1000 George Bush Drive
P.O. Box 10410
College Station, TX 77842-0410
409-260-9552

Clinton Presidential Materials Project
1000 LaHarpe Boulevard
Little Rock, AR 72201
501-254-6866

National Archives Regional Archives

NARA-Northeast Region
380 Trapelo Road
Waltham, MA 02452-6399
781-647-8104

NARA-Northeast Region
10 Conte Drive
Pittsfield, MA 01201-8230
413-445-6885

NARA-Northeast Region
201 Varick Street, 12th Floor
New York, NY 10014-4811
212-337-1300

NARA-Mid Atlantic Region
900 Market Street
Philadelphia, PA 19107-4292
215-597-3000

NARA-Mid Atlantic Region
14700 Townsend Road
Philadelphia, PA 19154-1096
215-671-9027

NARA-Southeast Region
1557 St. Joseph Avenue
East Point, GA 30344-2593
404-763-7474

NARA-Great Lakes Region
7358 South Pulaski Road
Chicago, IL 60629-5898
773-581-7816

NARA-Great Lakes Region
3150 Springboro Road
Dayton, OH 45439-1883
937-225-2852

NARA-Central Plains Region
2312 East Bannister Road
Kansas City, MO 64131-3011
816-926-6272

NARA-Central Plains Region
200 Space Center Drive
Lee's Summit, MO 64064-1182
816-478-7079

NARA-Southwest Region
501 West Felix Street
P.O. Box 6216
Fort Worth, TX 76115-0216
817-334-5525

NARA-Rocky Mountain Region
Denver Federal Center, Building 48
P.O. Box 25307
Denver, CO 80225-0307
303-236-0804

NARA-Pacific Region
24000 Avila Road
P.O. Box 6719
Laguna Niguel, CA 92607-6719
949-360-2641

NARA-Pacific Region
1000 Commodore Drive
San Bruno, CA 94066-2350
650-876-9009

NARA-Pacific Alaska Region
6125 Sand Point Way, NE
Seattle, WA 98115-7999
206-526-6507

NARA-Pacific Alaska Region
654 West Third Avenue
Anchorage, AK 99501-2145
907-271-2443

Reproductions of Documents

Reproductions of the oversized print documents included in these units are available in their original size by special order from Graphic Visions.

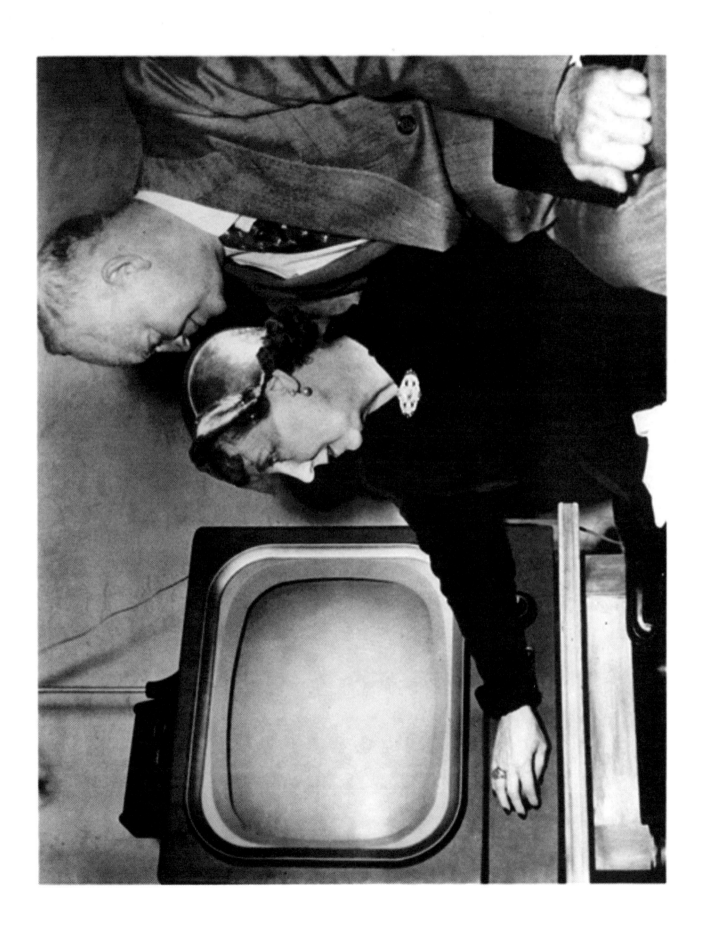

Document 1. Photograph of President Eisenhower and Mamie Eisenhower watching Richard Nixon's "Checkers speech" on television, September 23, 1952 (Dwight D. Eisenhower Presidential Library). © Wide World Photos, Inc. Used with permission. [National Archives]

Document 2. Photograph, "President Eisenhower, Roy Rogers, Dale Evans, and others attending grandson David Eisenhower's birthday party," March 31, 1956 (Dwight D. Eisenhower Presidential Library). [National Archives]

Document 3. Photograph, "President Eisenhower with Jane Powell, Bob Hope, Pearl Bailey, and others," June 7, 1956 (Dwight D. Eisenhower Presidential Library). [National Archives]

Document 4. Photograph, "President Eisenhower throwing out the ball for the opening game of the 1956 World Series," October 3, 1956 (Dwight D. Eisenhower Presidential Library). © by I.H.T. Corporation. Used with permission. [National Archives]

The Future of America

"THE BETTER YOU KNOW AMERICA…

THE BETTER THE FUTURE LOOKS"

Document 5a. The Advertising Council brochure entitled "The Future of America,"
1954 (Dwight D. Eisenhower Presidential Library). [National Archives]

LOOK INTO AMERICA'S

FUTURE...and you can see your own

Look into America's future, and you can set your hopes high.

This dynamic country of yours has been in a period of tremendous growth. This has meant more jobs, more money, more security, more homes and more opportunities for everyone.

As you look into the future, all that can be seen is promise of even greater growth for your country, and for you. This is the big promise, and the arithmetic that proves it is simple, dramatic, and as sure as two and two make four.

Since you opened this booklet, a baby has been born. By this time tomorrow, your country will have 11,000 new Americans. By next month, a city the size of Syracuse will have been added to the strength of your nation.

This is the secret! The almost unbelievable growth that can strengthen everybody's job, brighten everybody's opportunity, and assure everybody's future.

Turn these pages, and you'll see why . . .

Document 5b. The Advertising Council brochure entitled "The Future of America," 1954 (Dwight D. Eisenhower Presidential Library). [National Archives]

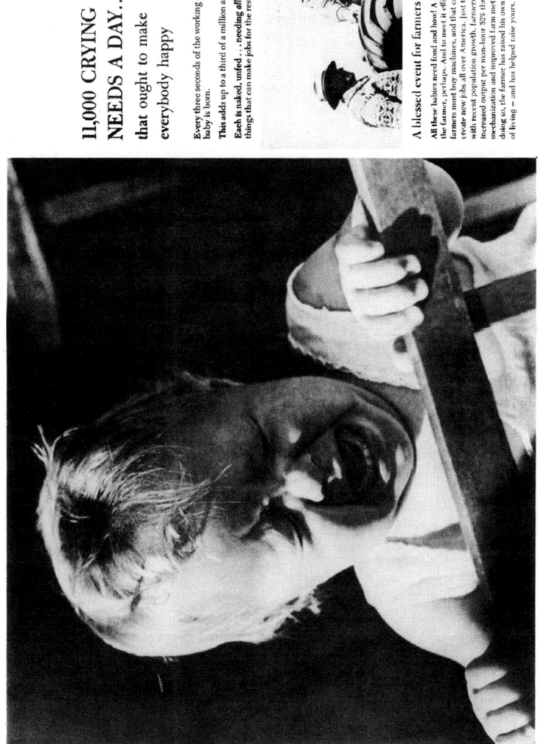

11,000 CRYING NEEDS A DAY...

that ought to make everybody happy

Every three seconds of the working day, a baby is born.

This adds up to a third of a million a month...

Each is naked, unfed...needing *all* of the things that can make jobs for the rest of us.

A blessed event for farmers and for you...

All these babies need food and how! A job first for the farmer, perhaps. And to meet it efficiently, farmers must buy machines, and that can help create new jobs all over America. Just to keep pace with recent population growth, farmers have increased output per man-hour 52% through mechanization and improved farm methods. In doing so, the farmer has raised his own standards of living — and has helped raise yours, too.

Document 5c. The Advertising Council brochure entitled "The Future of America," 1954 (Dwight D. Eisenhower Presidential Library). [National Archives]

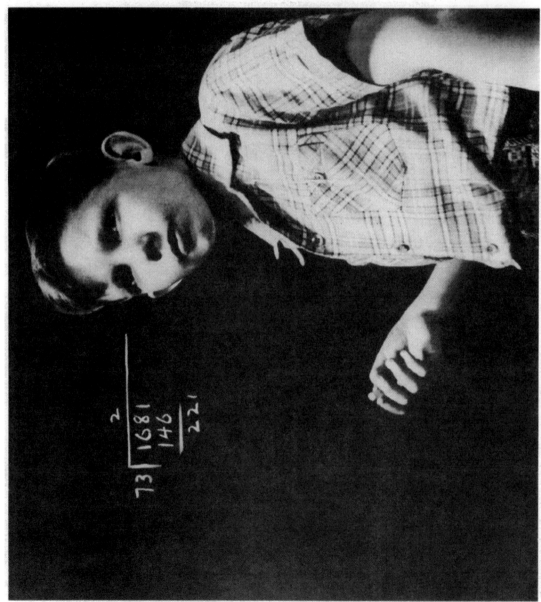

HE HAS A PROBLEM...

that can make work for millions

In America today, there are almost 70% more children under 5 years of age than we had in 1940.

This creates a tremendous need to build new schools. Billions of dollars worth of new schools are needed — because we must nearly *double* the existing system.

Abc's of a growing need . . .

It is estimated that we should spend some 40 billion dollars for schools and hospitals alone. And right away! Money spent in this construction creates work for bricklayers, masons, plumbers, architects, real estate brokers, construction workers and many others. In turn, everything they buy for themselves just adds new *UP* to everybody's opportunity for prosperity.

Document 5d. The Advertising Council brochure entitled "The Future of America," 1954 (Dwight D. Eisenhower Presidential Library). [National Archives]

THEY'RE OUTGROWING EVERYTHING...

including all our factories

Literally everything must grow faster and faster to keep up with the fantastic snowballing population growth ahead.

Business today faces an outlay of hundreds of billions of dollars just to modernize plants and replace worn out or outmoded machines. Future population growth will call for even greater investments — a dramatic challenge and opportunity that can mean good times ahead for everybody!

It takes energy just to keep up....

This tremendous backlog of needs that must be met does not even include the billions that the electrical industry needs to invest. Demand for electrical energy is expected to increase by 250% by 1975. Employees in this industry by the hundreds of thousands can be kept busy just trying to keep up with this need for growth.

Document 5e. The Advertising Council brochure entitled "The Future of America," 1954 (Dwight D. Eisenhower Presidential Library). [National Archives]

THEY'RE GOING NEW PLACES...
and so are you

The impact of this almost explosive growth is tremendous upon other industries, too.

Growth in population adds a brand new major city to the sales territory of businesses every month. The major problem is to keep up . . . to expand fast enough.

Highway transport, which employs one American in seven today, is one industry to benefit. Just two, for example, of the automobile manufacturers have immediate plans to spend over a billion and a quarter to expand, while just one oil company expects to spend $500 million.

Roads to prosperity . . .

Even without our new millions of babies we'd have to remodel our entire highway system right now . . . a 60 billion dollar enterprise that can mean almost unlimited opportunity for all directly or indirectly employed in highway construction industries. (This need is pressing, too, for today's roads are carrying 55 million vehicles, 72% more than in 1940.)

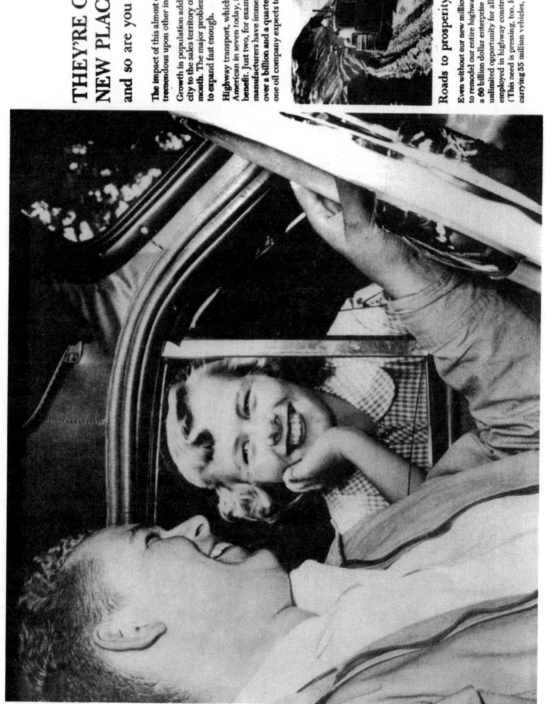

Document 5f. The Advertising Council brochure entitled "The Future of America,"
1954 (Dwight D. Eisenhower Presidential Library). [National Archives]

THEY STEP ACROSS THIS THRESHOLD . . .

and the bells of the nation's cash register ring!

We're adding new families to our nation faster than ever before, as yesterday's bumper crops of babies come to altar age.

A larger proportion of our adult population is married than ever before, and people marry younger and have larger families.

The wedding present for everybody!

New families need homes (and everything that goes into them)! Since 1950, we have built three million new homes. But this is not nearly enough. 67% of our homes are now over twenty years old. 50% are over thirty years old. Right now we need 100 billion dollars worth of new homes. If your family's livelihood depends on making or selling anything for house-building or house-furnishing or house re-modeling . . . *the only trend that can be seen ahead is up.*

Document 5g. The Advertising Council brochure entitled "The Future of America," 1954 (Dwight D. Eisenhower Presidential Library). [National Archives]

BANK ACCOUNTS GROW AS FAMILIES GROW...

and we're the best off nation in the world

Americans have, in spite of inflation, over *twice* the spending power today that we had in 1940. Savings have risen from $68.5 billion in 1940 to an estimated $250 billion today.

The long range trend in employment is *up.* Even though employment in some areas has fallen off, we still have twenty million more jobs than we had in 1939.

Greater horizons for bigger families...

American science continues to give us miraculous developments in electronics, jets, rockets, chemistry, which are opening broad new fields of opportunity. *We stand at the very beginning of the new atomic world.* And this alone may be the most tremendous personal and industrial opportunity of all time. Millions of today's youngsters can prosper in jobs that parents have never even heard of right now.

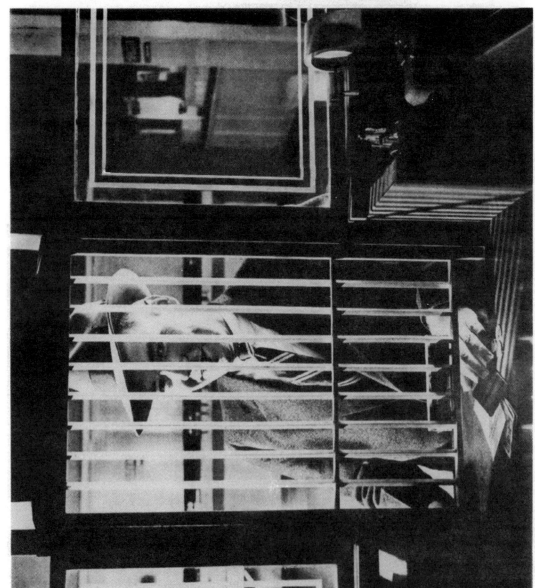

Document 5h. The Advertising Council brochure entitled "The Future of America," 1954 (Dwight D. Eisenhower Presidential Library). [National Archives]

THEY TAKE IT EASY...

and make more jobs

**Not only are more people getting married ...
and having more children ... but our people
are *living longer*.**

By 1960 our population over 65 years old will
number over fifteen and a half million people –
more than the entire population of Canada.

And today, old people are more active, travel
more, and have more money to spend.

Old age benefits for everybody...

Resorts, steamships, motels, and a host of small
businesses are already benefiting. An opportunity
of unprecedented scope can open up for our vast
and varied entertainment industries ... an
opportunity enormously increased by the greater
leisure time of young and old alike. For instance,
forty million Americans get paid vacations *today*.

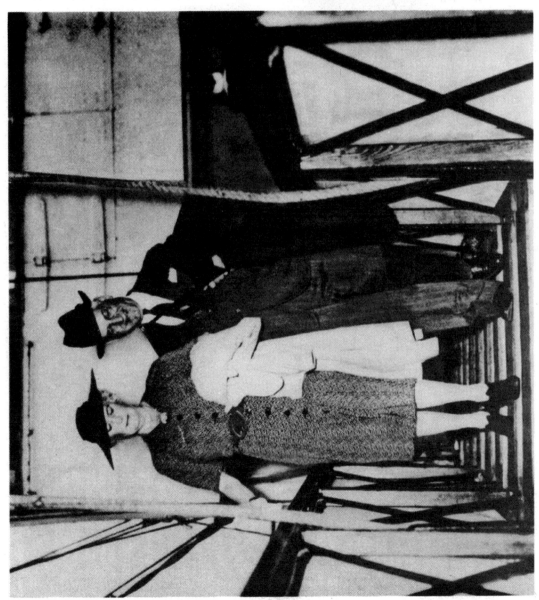

Document 5i. The Advertising Council brochure entitled "The Future of America,"
1954 (Dwight D. Eisenhower Presidential Library). [National Archives]

It all adds up to a...

$500,000,000,000

OPPORTUNITY RIGHT NOW...

because this staggering sum should be spent immediately *just to meet current actual needs.*

This calls for the *greatest* individual and industrial effort in peacetime history.

It can mean work of all kinds for *everybody.*

And the tremendous job of keeping up with future population growth is *still ahead.*

No matter who you are—no matter how you make a living—you, as an American, can *set your hopes high.*

Document 5j. The Advertising Council brochure entitled "The Future of America," 1954 (Dwight D. Eisenhower Presidential Library). [National Archives]

THE BETTER
YOU KNOW
AMERICA...
THE BETTER
THE FUTURE
LOOKS

Document 5k. The Advertising Council brochure entitled "The Future of America,"
1954 (Dwight D. Eisenhower Presidential Library). [National Archives]

This booklet is part of a public information

program conducted by The Advertising Council, Inc., in the interest of a better-informed and hence a stronger America.

The Advertising Council is a non-profit, non-political, non-partisan organization formed to utilize advertising in the public service. Established shortly after Pearl Harbor, the Council helped plan and prepare, without charge, advertising for such World War II programs as War Bonds, Food Conservation, Scrap Salvage, Paper Salvage and over 100 others.

In these critical times the Council is devoting its energies to many information programs in the national welfare and in the interest of a free world.

Advertising on Council programs is prepared through the generosity of leading American advertising agencies. American business donates, as a public service, the advertising time and space in magazines, radio, television, newspapers, outdoor posters and car cards.

The Council conducts only those programs which derive their authority from an Act of Congress or which in the absence of such an Act are determined, by its Board of Directors and by a Public Policy Committee of 20 distinguished citizens, to serve the best interests of all Americans.

(For prices of this booklet in quantity lots, write: The Advertising Council, Inc., 25 West 45th Street, New York 36, New York)

This booklet was prepared for The Advertising Council by McCann-Erickson, Inc. as a public service.

Statistics were largely derived from the following sources: U. S. Department of Commerce • U. S. Department of Labor • American Medical Association Journal • U. S. Office of Education • 1953 Yearbook of American Churches • Federal Security Agency • U. S. Department of Agriculture • Federal Reserve Board

Document 6. Photograph, "Senator Joseph R. McCarthy," March 14, 1950. [National Archives]

Supreme Court of the United States

No. 1 ———, October Term, 19 54

Oliver Brown, Mrs. Richard Lawton, Mrs. Sadie Emmanuel et al.,

Appellants,

vs.

Board of Education of Topeka, Shawnee County, Kansas, et al.

Appeal from the United States District Court for the ————————————— District of Kansas.

This cause came on to be heard on the transcript of the record from the United States District Court for the —————————— District of Kansas, ————————————— and was argued by counsel.

On consideration whereof, It is ordered and adjudged by this Court that the judgment of the said District ————————————— Court in this cause be, and the same is hereby, reversed with costs; and that this cause be, and the same is hereby, remanded to the said District Court to take such proceedings and enter such orders and decrees consistent with the opinions of this Court as are necessary and proper to admit to public schools on a racially nondiscriminatory basis with all deliberate speed the parties to this case.

Per Mr. Chief Justice Warren,

May 31, 1955.

Document 7. Enabling decision in *Brown v. Board of Education of Topeka, Kansas*, May 31, 1955. [National Archives]

FOR RELEASE AT 9:00 P.M. EDT, SEPTEMBER 24, 1957

James C. Hagerty, Press Secretary to the President

-- --

THE WHITE HOUSE

TEXT OF THE ADDRESS BY THE PRESIDENT
OF THE UNITED STATES, DELIVERED FROM
HIS OFFICE AT THE WHITE HOUSE, TUESDAY,
SEPTEMBER 24, 1957, AT 9:00 P.M. EDT

My Fellow Citizens:

For a few minutes I want to speak to you about the serious
situation that has arisen in Little Rock.   For this talk I have come
to the President's office in the White House.   I could have spoken
from Rhode Island, but I felt that, in speaking from the house of
Lincoln, of Jackson and of Wilson, my words would more clearly
convey both the sadness I feel in the action I was compelled today
to take and the firmness with which I intend to pursue this course
until the orders of the Federal Court at Little Rock can be
executed without unlawful interference.

In that city, under the leadership of demagogic extremists,
disorderly mobs have deliberately prevented the carrying out of
proper orders from a Federal Court. Local authorities have
not eliminated that violent opposition and, under the law, I
yesterday issued a Proclamation calling upon the mob to disperse.

This morning the mob again gathered in front of the
Central High School of Little Rock, obviously for the purpose
of again preventing the carrying out of the Court's order relating
to the admission of Negro children to the school.

Whenever normal agencies prove inadequate to the task
and it becomes necessary for the Executive Branch of the Federal
Government to use its powers and authority to uphold Federal
Courts, the President's responsibility is inescapable.

In accordance with that responsibility, I have today issued
an Executive Order directing the use of troops under Federal
authority to aid in the execution of Federal law at Little Rock,
Arkansas. This became necessary when my Proclamation of
yesterday was not observed, and the obstruction of justice still
continues.

It is important that the reasons for my action be understood
by all citizens.

As you know, the Supreme Court of the United States has
decided that separate public educational facilities for the races
are inherently unequal and therefore compulsory school segregation
laws are unconstitutional.

more

Document 8a. Text of Presidential address released to the
press regarding the Little Rock crisis, September 24, 1957
(Dwight D. Eisenhower Presidential Library). [National Archives]

Our personal opinions about the decision have no bearing on the matter of enforcement; the responsibility and authority of the Supreme Court to interpret the Constitution are clear. Local Federal Courts were instructed by the Supreme Court to issue such orders and decrees as might be necessary to achieve admission to public schools without regard to race -- and with all deliberate speed.

During the past several years, many communities in our Southern States have instituted public school plans for gradual progress in the enrollment and attendance of school children of all races in order to bring themselves into compliance with the law of the land.

They thus demonstrated to the world that we are a nation in which laws, not men, are supreme.

I regret to say that this truth -- the cornerstone of our liberties -- was not observed in this instance.

It was my hope that this localized situation would be brought under control by city and State authorities. If the use of local police powers had been sufficient, our traditional method of leaving the problem in those hands would have been pursued. But when large gatherings of obstructionists made it impossible for the decrees of the Court to be carried out, both the law and the national interest demanded that the President take action.

Here is the sequence of events in the development of the Little Rock school case.

In May of 1955, the Little Rock School Board approved a moderate plan for the gradual desegregation of the public schools in that city. It provided that a start toward integration would be made at the present term in the high school, and that the plan would be in full operation by 1963. This plan was challenged in the courts by some who believed that the period of time as proposed was too long.

The United States Court at Little Rock, which has supervisory responsibility under the law for the plan of desegregation in the public schools, dismissed the challenge, thus approving a gradual rather than an abrupt change from the existing system. It found that the school board had acted in good faith in planning for a public school system free from racial discrimination.

Since that time, the court has on three separate occasions issued orders directing that the plan be carried out. All persons were instructed to refrain from interfering with the efforts of the school board to comply with the law.

Proper and sensible observance of the law then demanded the respectful obedience which the nation has a right to expect from all the people. This, unfortunately, has not been the case at Little Rock. Certain misguided persons, many of them imported into Little Rock by agitators, have insisted upon defying the law and have sought to bring it into disrepute. The orders of the court have thus been frustrated.

more

Document 8b. Text of Presidential address released to the press regarding the Little Rock crisis, September 24, 1957 (Dwight D. Eisenhower Presidential Library). [National Archives]

The very basis of our individual rights and freedoms is the certainty that the President and the Executive Branch of Government will support and insure the carrying out of the decisions of the Federal Courts, even, when necessary with all the means at the President's command.

Unless the President did so, anarchy would result.

There would be no security for any except that which each one of us could provide for himself.

The interest of the nation in the proper fulfillment of the law's requirements cannot yield to opposition and demonstrations by some few persons.

Mob rule cannot be allowed to override the decisions of the courts.

Let me make it very clear that Federal troops are not being used to relieve local and state authorities of their primary duty to preserve the peace and order of the community. Nor are the troops there for the purpose of taking over the responsibility of the School Board and the other repsonsible local officials in running Central High School. In the present case the troops are there, pursuant to law, solely for the purpose of preventing interference with the orders of the Court.

The proper use of the powers of the Executive Branch to enforce the orders of a Federal Court is limited to extraordinary and compelling circumstances. Manifestly, such an extreme situation has been created in Little Rock. This challenge must be met with such measures as will preserve to the people as a whole their lawfully-protected rights in a climate permitting their free and fair exercise.

The overwhelming majority of our people in every section of the country are united in their respect for observance of the law -- even in those cases where they may disagree with that law.

They deplore the call of extremists to violence.

The decision of the Supreme Court concerning school integration affects the South more seriously than it does other sections of the country. In that region I have many warm friends, some of them in the city of Little Rock. I have deemed it a great personal privilege to spend in our Southland tours of duty while in the military service and enjoyable recreational periods since that time.

So from intimate personal knowledge, I know that the overwhelming majority of the people in the South -- including those of Arkansas and of Little Rock -- are of good will, united in their efforts to preserve and respect the law even when they disagree with it.

more

Document 8c. Text of Presidential address released to the press regarding the Little Rock crisis, September 24, 1957 (Dwight D. Eisenhower Presidential Library). [National Archives]

They do not sympathize with mob rule. They, like the rest of the nation, have proved in two great wars their readiness to sacrifice for America.

A foundation of our American way of life is our national respect for law.

In the South, as elsewhere, citizens are keenly aware of the tremendous disservice that has been done to the people of Arkansas in the eyes of the nation, and that has been done to the nation in the eyes of the world.

At a time when we face a grave situation abroad because of the hatred that Communism bears toward a system of government based on human rights, it would be difficult to exaggerate the harm that is being done to the prestige and influence, and indeed to the safety, of our nation and the world.

Our enemies are gloating over this incident and using it everywhere to misrepresent our nation. We are portrayed as a violator of those standards of conduct which the peoples of the world united to proclaim in the Charter of the United Nations. There they affirmed "faith in fundamental human rights and in the dignity of the human person" and did so "without distinction as to race, sex, language ar religion."

And so, with confidence, I call upon citizens of the State of Arkansas to assist in bringing to an immediate end all interference with the law and its processes. If resistance to the Federal Court orders ceases at once, the further presence of Federal troops will be unnecessary and the City of Little Rock will return to its normal habits of peace and order and a blot upon the fair name and high honor of our nation in the world will be removed.

Thus will be restored the image of America and of all its parts as one nation, indivisible, with liberty and justice for all.

########

85TH CONGRESS
1ST SESSION

H. R. 6127

[Report No. 291]

IN THE HOUSE OF REPRESENTATIVES

MARCH 19, 1957

Mr. CELLER introduced the following bill; which was referred to the Committee on the Judiciary

APRIL 1, 1957

Committed to the Committee of the Whole House on the State of the Union and ordered to be printed

---

A BILL

To provide means of further securing and protecting the civil rights of persons within the jurisdiction of the United States

1   *Be it enacted by the Senate and House of Representa-*

2   *tives of the United States of America in Congress assembled,*

3   PART I—ESTABLISHMENT OF THE COMMISSION ON CIVIL

4   RIGHTS

5   SEC. 101. (a) There is created in the executive branch

6   of the Government a Commission on Civil Rights (herein-

7   after called the "Commission").

8   (b) The Commission shall be composed of six mem-

9   bers who shall be appointed by the President by and with

10 the advice and consent of the Senate. Not more than three

I

CIVIL RIGHTS

APRIL 1, 1957.—Committed to the Committee of the Whole House on the State of the Union and ordered to be printed

Mr. RODINO, from the Committee on the Judiciary, submitted the following

REPORT

[To accompany H. R. 6127]

The Committee on the Judiciary, to whom was referred the bill (H. R. 6127) to provide means of further securing and protecting the civil rights of persons within the jurisdiction of the United States, having considered the same, report favorably thereon without amendment and recommend that the bill do pass.

PURPOSE OF THE BILL

The bill is designed to protect the civil rights of persons within the jurisdiction of the United States. In order to accomplish that objective, the bill provides the establishment of a bipartisan commission to investigate asserted violations of law in the field of civil rights which involve the right to vote and to make studies and recommendations of the legal developments and policies of the Federal Government with respect to the equal protection of laws under the Constitution of the United States. It also provides for an additional Assistant Attorney General, who would be in charge of a Civil Rights Division in the Department of Justice. The bill amends existing law so as to permit the Federal Government to seek from the civil courts preventive or other necessary relief in civil-rights cases. Finally, it proposes the enactment of new laws to assist in the enforcement of the right to vote.

HISTORY OF THE LEGISLATION

The Committee on the Judiciary had referred to it 60 bills dealing with civil rights; these bills touched upon the various aspects of the subject matter, including such topics as antilynching, peonage, kidnaping, crimes involving civil rights, segregation, voting, fair-employment practices, creation of a Civil Rights Commission, of a Joint

86006—57——1

Congressional Committee on Civil Rights, and of a Civil Rights Division in the Department of Justice.

While a subcommittee conducted hearings on all of those bills, its attention was concentrated mainly on two bills, H. R. 1151 and H. R. 2145, introduced by Representatives Keating and Celler, respectively. Those two bills were substantially similar although the latter bill contained additional proposals which related to criminal sanctions.

The hearings were held on February 4, 5, 6, 7, 13, 14, 25, and 26, 1957, and printed as Serial No. 1, Civil Rights, hearings before Subcommittee No. 5 of the Committee on the Judiciary, House of Representatives, 85th Congress, 1st session, 1,299 pages. In addition to the testimony taken on the above dates, the hearings conducted by a Judiciary subcommittee in the 84th Congress on similar legislation were made part of the record.

The witnesses who appeared at the hearings represented all the various interests concerned with the legislation. Besides the congressional authors of the bills, the Attorney General of the United States testified, as did representatives of various private organizations which support civil-rights legislation. Among the witnesses who appeared in opposition to the legislation were Members of both Houses of Congress, State officials, attorneys general—some being represented by counsel—members of various State legislatures and judiciaries and also representatives of private groups and organizations which oppose the enactment of the legislation. The subcommittee endeavored to grant all persons who could contribute constructively to the problem the opportunity to be heard; it knows of no person or group who was denied a reasonable opportunity to testify or present relevant material on the pending proposals.

After the hearing had been concluded, the subcommittee proceeded to consider the bill H. R. 2145; it struck from the bill all the matter it contained and inserted the proposals contained in H. R. 1151. While the same substantive proposals had been part of H. R. 2145, there was a slight difference in language and form. Moreover, the criminal sanctions contained in H. R. 2145 were deleted.

Other amendments to the proposed bill H. R. 2145 were made by the subcommittee, mainly as a result of testimony and evidence adduced at the hearings. Since a detailed analysis of the bill is set forth in this report, a mere mention of the amendments should suffice at this point. The subcommittee inserted into the bills rules of procedure for the Commission, limitations on the Commission's subpena power were established to prevent abuse; complaints to the Commission are to be written and verified; religion was deleted as a category upon which discrimination could be predicated and finally the written consent of the aggrieved party was made a condition precedent in an action to recover damages by the Attorney General of the United States.

The bill then recommended by the subcommittee to the full Judiciary Committee contained the four major proposals as set forth in this report under the purpose of the bill, as amended by the proposals outlined in the above paragraphs:

The full Judiciary Committee, in its deliberations and consideration of the amended bill, H. R. 2145, adopted the four major proposals, namely, the creation of the Commission on Civil Rights, the establishment of a Civil Rights Division in the Department of Justice,

supplement to title 42, United States Code, section 1985, providing civil remedies against conspiracies depriving a person of civil rights and provision for a civil remedy by the Attorney General to strengthen and protect the right to vote.

Aside from certain technical amendments involving changes in language and form, the Judiciary Committee approved the proposal of the subcommittee with the following substantive changes: Made it a crime to disclose evidence taken in an executive session without the consent of the Commission; raised to $12 per day the subsistence allowance of a witness; eliminated as a duty of the Commission the investigation of allegations of unwarranted economic pressures being used as a means of discrimination, but authorized the Commission to investigate a deprivation of the right to vote because of religion, as well as others; limited the duty of the Commission to study and collect only the legal developments, constituting a denial of equal protection of the laws under the Constitution, thus deleting the social and economic aspects of the same problem; waived the conflict of interests statute for members of the Commission and voluntary and uncompensated personnel; required a showing of reasonable grounds of belief that a person is about to engage in an act before restraintive or preventative relief may be granted in suits involving title 42. United States Code, section 1985, or the right to vote; finally, the provision permitting the Attorney General to bring suit to recover damages for an aggrieved party because of a deprivation of civil rights or the right to vote was eliminated, thus limiting the Attorney General in such cases to civil actions for injunctive relief.

The committee then approved H. R. 2145 as amended but ordered the chairman to introduce a clean bill embodying its approved proposals. This was done and the committee then ordered reported favorably the bill H. R. 6127—the clean bill introduced by the chairman at the direction of the committee.

On July 23, 1956, the House of Representatives passed the bill H. R. 627 but no action was taken on that proposal in the Senate. As H. R. 627 passed the House, it was substantially similar to the bill H. R. 6127 as reported here insofar as the four basic and major provisions are concerned. They are the provisions for the creation of a Commission on Civil Rights and of a Civil Rights Division in the Department of Justice and provisions to supplement and strengthen existing statutes involving conspiracies depriving one of civil rights and the right to vote by authorizing the Attorney General to initiate civil actions for injunctive relief in those types of cases.

There are, however, certain differences between H. R. 627 of the 84th Congress and H. R. 6127 as reported in the 85th Congress. The major differences of a substantive nature relate to rule of procedure for the Commission; another is that the provisions of H. R. 6127 place limitations on the subpena power of the Commission which were not contained in H. R. 627. Still another is found in H. R. 6127 whereby willful and unauthorized disclosure of evidence obtained in an executive session of the Commission is made a crime; H. R. 627 had no such provision.

One of the major variations of those two bills is the elimination from H. R. 6127 of the duty of the Commission to investigate allegations of unwarranted economic pressure being brought to bear on persons because of race, color, religion, or national origin. Such a duty was imposed on the Commission by H. R. 627. H. R. 6127 also required that allegations of complaints filed with the Commission must be in writing and verified, whereas H. R. 627 merely required them to be in writing. H. R. 6127 imposes upon the Commission the duty to study and collect information concerning the legal developments constituting a denial of equal protection of the laws under the Constitution, but H. R. 627 had included the economic and social aspects of the same subject matter.

H. R. 627, as it passed the House, included in the duties of the Commission the responsibility to inquire into illegal voting and also into discrimination by reason of sex. Neither of those matters are contained in H. R. 6127.

H. R. 627 placed no restriction on the utilization by the Commission of voluntary uncompensated personnel nor were the conflict-of-interest statutes waived for such persons and the members of the Commission, but H. R. 6127 limits such personnel to 15 at any one time and also waives the conflict-of-interest laws.

Another major difference between the two bills involves the authorization for the Attorney General to institute civil actions in certain cases involving title 42, United States Code, section 1985—deprivation of certain civil rights—and section 1971—voting rights. Under H. R. 627 the Attorney General could bring a civil action in the name of the United States but for the benefit of the real party in interest to recover damages as well as other preventive relief. H. R. 6127 eliminates that authority to recover and permits such civil suits to those for or in the name of the United States for proper injunctive relief.

GENERAL STATEMENT

The history of the United States of America is a running story of the continuing struggle to achieve the goal which our Founding Fathers recognized in the expression "that all men are created equal, that they are endowed by their Creator with certain Unalienable rights, that among these are Life, Liberty and the pursuit of Happiness."

The rights and privileges of all Americans are the responsibility of the Federal Government because those rights and privileges are anchored in the Constitution and laws of the United States; they are attributes of national citizenship which recognize the dignity of the human being as the true basic reason for the very existence of government itself. Under our American concept of government, the consent of the governed is the sole source of political authority.

Although our record as a nation is definitely one of progress toward the achievement of the ideal for which this Government was established, it would not be proper to permit stagnation at any point prior to reaching, as far as humanly possible, the true American way of life. As human brings subject to the frailties of our nature, perfection is something that is never achieved but must be honestly and conscientiously striven for during every moment of our existence. Moreover, any halt in the constant struggle would be a betrayal of the national conscience of America which seeks equality for all under the law. As Americans, we must also realize and accept the fact that the responsibility of worldwide leadership carries with it a concomitant duty of providing the world with examples of freedom and liberty for

all in our daily lives. Any intolerance or discrimination or deprivation of our constitutionally guaranteed rights and privileges resound and reverberate throughout the globe. But more important than even these worldwide ramifications is the right and the duty of the Government to fulfill its responsibility to each and every American citizen.

Who but the Federal Government should be the leading example in shouldering the burdens for which it was created? In the field of civil rights, the Federal Government must assume the ultimate responsibility for the protection of individuals when State and local enforcement and protection of such rights fail.

The need for legislation such as proposed by the bill H. R. 6127 has, in the opinion of the majority of the members of the committee, been clearly established. In support of such a contention are the report of the President's Committee on Civil Rights in 1947, the message of President Truman in 1948, and the messages of President Eisenhower in 1956 and on January 10, 1957, and corroborating those recommendations is that of the Attorney General of the United States as contained in an executive communication of April 9, 1956, which was repeated again during the course of his testimony before the committee in 1957. The provisions of the bill H. R. 6127 are designed to achieve a more effective enforcement of the rights already guaranteed by the Constitution and laws of the United States. This is particularly true with regard to the right of franchise in Federal matters. Moreover, the bill reflects what the committee believes to be the desire of the American people to continue to expand our American concept of freedom. That is done by the creation of a Commission on Civil Rights for the purpose of investigation and study of a denial of a right to vote because of race, creed, color, or racial origin and to analyze the legal developments in Federal policies and laws involving the constitutional right of equal protection under the laws.

The hearings before the committee indicated the need for what has been termed a "necessary minimum". Moreover, it has been demonstrated to the committee that the problem is not a provincial one but a national problem. The scope of the bill is that of the entire nation and is not directed at nor motivated by any sectional interest. Because the problem is a continuing one, and because the committee believes that the American body politic seeks progress toward equality for all and equal protection of the laws for all, the Commission is authorized to make a study upon which to base its recommendations for future, if any, legislation in the field of civil rights. While there may or may not be in a need for additional legislation, there can be no denial of the fact that there is an existing need for an immediate strengthening of the enforcement of existing rights. For that reason, the bill permits the creation of a Civil Rights Division in the Department of Justice and confers upon the Attorney General of the United States the authority to institute civil actions in the name of the United States or for the United States to protect the existing rights and to expand the right of franchise in Federal elections.

It is the opinion of the Committee on the Judiciary that the proposed legislation neither encroaches upon nor diminishes the respective powers of a State or the Federal Government as recognized in the American concept of dual sovereignty. The proposal does not extend nor increase the area of civil rights jurisdiction in which the Federal Government is entitled to act. Those rights are presently protected by constitutional amendment and when violations occur they are subject to Federal prosecution. The provisions of the legislation, in fact, merely substitute civil proceedings for criminal proceedings in the already established field.

With regard to the proposals involving the right to vote, the Federal Government has placed upon it by article I, section 4, of the Constitution the authority to regulate the manner of conducting elections and that authority is further supplemented by the 14th and 15th amendments. Of course, such authority is limited to elections for Federal office, but the 15th amendment denies the right of any State to abridge or deny the right to vote because of race, color, or previous condition of servitude. Also, the 14th amendment operates to prevent any State from enacting or enforcing a law which would abridge the privilege and immunity of a United States citizen and denying such a person the equal protection of the laws. These two amendments expressly authorize Congress to enforce them by legislation.

The remaining provisions of the legislation relate to the jurisdiction of the Federal Government in the field of existing civil rights. The Commission created by the proposal is purely investigatory and empowered only to make recommendations. The other provision relating to a Civil Rights Division in the Department of Justice concerns only the Federal Government. Thus, for the above reasons, it is believed that any fear of interference by the Federal Government in the traditional rights of a State are wholly unwarranted and unfounded.

A SECTIONAL ANALYSIS OF THE LEGISLATION

PART I—ESTABLISHMENT OF THE COMMISSION ON CIVIL RIGHTS

Section 101 of the bill creates a six-man bipartisan Commission on Civil Rights in the executive branch of the Government. Members of the Commission are to be appointed by the President and confirmed by the Senate. The chairman and vice chairman are to be designated by the President and a quorum is fixed as four members.

Section 102 contains the rules of procedure of the Commission. The rules require an opening statement on the part of the chairman as to the subject matter of the hearing. Witnesses before the Commission must be furnished with a copy of the rules and are entitled to be represented by counsel. The chairman is authorized to discipline the meeting and to banish counsel for breaches of decorum, order, and unprofessional ethics.

Whenever the Commission finds that a person may be defamed, degraded, or incriminated by reason of testimony or evidence presented at a hearing, it must, receive such evidence or testimony in executive session and afford such person an opportunity to appear as a voluntary witness. If requests are made of the Commission to subpena additional witnesses, it is within the authority of the Commission to consider and dispose of such requests. Evidence of testimony acquired in executive session can only be released or used in public sessions with the consent of the Commission. Any willful and unauthorized disclosure is subject to criminal prosecution with punishment of a fine of not more than $1,000 or imprisonment for not more

than a year. Brief and pertinent sworn written statements may be inserted in the record before the Commission, which is the sole judge of the pertinency of testimony and evidence adduced at its hearings. Transcripts of the hearings may be purchased by a witness and, if given in executive session, when authorized by the Commission. Provision is made for paying a witness $4 a day for attendance at and traveling to and from the place of hearing; the mileage reimbursement from his home is fixed at a rate of 8 cents per mile. If attendance is required for more than a day, the witness is entitled to an additional allowance of $12 per day for subsistence expenses, including necessary travel time. Payment for travel must be tendered the witness whenever a subpena is served on behalf of the Commission or any subcommittee. A person subpenaed by the Commission cannot be required to attend if his presence as a witness would be outside the geographic limits of the judicial circuit of the United States wherein the witness had been found, resided, or transacted business.

Section 103 fixes the compensation of a member of the Commission who is not in the service of the Federal Government at $50 per day for each day devoted to the work of the Commission and necessary and actual travel expenses are reimbursable as well as a per diem allowance of $12 in lieu of actual expenses. Any member of the Commission who is in the service of the Government of the United States is not entitled to compensation other than that which he receives for such other service. But such a person may be reimbursed for actual and necessary travel expenses and is allowed a per diem allowance of $12 in lieu of actual expenses for subsistence.

Section 104 sets forth the duties of the Commission. The Commission is empowered to investigate deprivation of the right of citizens of the United States to vote by reason of their color, race, religion or national origin. Such allegations, however, must be in writing and under oath or affirmation and shall set forth the facts upon which such belief is predicated.

The second duty imposed upon the Commission is to study and collect information relating to the legal developments which constitute a denial of equal protection of the laws under the Constitution.

The third duty requires the appraisal of the laws and policies of the Federal Government with respect to equal protection of the laws under the Constitution.

The Commission is authorized to submit to the President interim reports whenever it deems fit, or when called upon by the President. The bill requires a final report of the Commission's work and recommendations no later than 2 years from the date of the enactment of this act. Sixty days after submission of the final report the Commission shall cease to exist.

Section 105 sets forth the powers of the Commission. It authorizes the employment of a full-time staff director and such other personnel as the Commission deems necessary. Employment must be in accordance with civil service and classification laws, and it may employ on a temporary basis experts or consultants in accordance with section 15 of the act of August 2, 1946 (60 Stat. 810; 5 U.S.C. 55 (a)). The rate of compensation for such individuals may not exceed $50 per day. The Commission is authorized to utilize the services of voluntary and uncompensated personnel and to reimburse them for travel and subsistence while engaged in the work of the Commission. Provision is made, however, that not more than 15 persons may be employed in such capacity at any one time. It is the opinion of the committee also that the Commission should not employ at any one time more than half of this type of personnel who are affiliated with the same organization or group.

Provision is made for the Commission to establish advisory committees and to consult with local and State representatives such as governors, attorney generals, and other State or local officials, as well as representatives and members of private organizations.

Waiver of the conflict-of-interest statutes is provided for members of the Commission as well as voluntary and uncompensated personnel. The cooperation of Federal agencies with the Commission in order that it may carry out its functions and duties is authorized.

The Commission, or upon the authorization of the Commission, subcommittees of at least two or more members, at least one of whom must be of each major political party, may hold such hearings and act at such times and places as deemed advisable. Subpenas may be issued over the signature of the Chairman of the Commission or of the subcommittee and service may be made by anyone designated by such chairman.

In the case of contumacy or refusal to obey a subpena, the Attorney General of the United States is authorized to apply to a United States district court or a United States court of any Territory or possession wherein the inquiry is carried on or within whose jurisdiction the person guilty of contumacy or refusal to obey is found or resides or transacts business, for an order requiring appearance before the Commission or its subcommittee. Failure to obey such an order of the court may be punished by the court as a contempt thereof.

Section 106 authorizes an appropriation of moneys, not otherwise appropriated, as may be necessary to carry out the provisions of the act.

The need for the creation of a Civil Rights Commission as provided in title I of the bill is to be found in the very nature of the problem involved; the complexity of the subject matter demands greater knowledge and understanding of every facet of the problem. For that reason, the proposal creates a factfinding and investigatory body. Its primary purpose is to collect and accumulate data so that a more intelligent study of the problem may be made. At the present time there is no agency in the executive branch of the Government with the authority to accomplish the objective for which the Commission is to be created. The subject matter which the Commission is directed to investigate and study is beyond the authority of the Federal Bureau of Investigation. The subject matter, at the same time, many governmental agencies are compiling daily information on almost every aspect of our lives. It is believed that the creation of this Commission will fill that vacuum and that its recommendation will result in a more intelligent understanding and approach to this vital problem. Presidents Truman and Eisenhower have advocated such a Commission and the present Attorney General has recommended it.

PART II—PROVISION FOR AN ADDITIONAL ASSISTANT ATTORNEY GENERAL

Section 111 of the bill authorizes the appointment by the President, with the advice and consent of the Senate, an additional Assistant Attorney General under the supervision of the Attorney General.

While the bill does not specify that the additional Assistant Attorney General authorized by section 111 shall be the head of a Civil Rights Division in the Department of Justice, it is the understanding of the committee, predicated upon testimony of the Attorney General, that the individual authorized to be employed by this section will be so designated and given such responsibility. The reason for not specifically stating the title and duties of the newly authorized assistant is purely one of internal management on the part of the Attorney General as head of the Department of Justice.

At present there is in the Department of Justice as part of the Criminal Division a section known as the Civil Rights Section. It was first created in 1939. Its function and purpose has been to direct, supervise, and conduct criminal prosecutions of violations of the laws and Constitution of the United States guaranteeing individual civil rights. It is also charged with enforcement of the criminal provisions of the Fair Labor Standards Act (29 U. S. C. 201, et seq.), the penalty provisions of the Safety Appliances Act, relating to railroads (45 U. S. C. 1, et seq.), the Kickback Act (18 U. S. C. 874), and certain statutes relating to elections.

However, it is no longer logical that this section should remain as a subdivision of the Criminal Division since recently the Justice Department has been obliged to engage in activities of a civil nature in the civil rights field. Typical examples is the litigation arising out of the situations in Hoxie, Ark., and Clinton, Tenn. Moreover, the adoption by Congress of the proposals as contained in parts III and IV of the bill would increase the volume of litigation in which the Department of Justice would be involved.

Probably the most important factor providing for such a Division is the fact that the problems which arise in the area of civil rights are extremely complex and very delicate in nature. The problem touches the very essence of Federal-State relationship and, therefore, requires a centralized responsibility in the person of an eminently qualified attorney with the prestige of a Presidential appointment behind him. The responsibility of such a position demands complete attention at all times to the many and varied aspects of the civil rights program as it exists under Federal jurisdiction. The creation of this position has received the same endorsement and recommendations as has the creation of the Commission on Civil Rights. The salary of the position would be commensurate with that of other Assistant Attorneys General; namely, $20,000 annually.

PART III—TO STRENGTHEN THE CIVIL RIGHTS STATUTES, AND FOR OTHER PURPOSES

Section 121 amends title 42, United States Code, section 1985 (sec. 1980 of the Revised Statutes) by adding two new paragraphs at the end thereof. The first of the new paragraphs provides that the Attorney General may institute for the United States or in the name of the United States a civil action for preventive relief whenever a person has committed any acts or practices which would give rise to a cause of action under the existing law as contained in section 1985. It further provides that the United States shall be liable for costs the same as a private person. The second new paragraph confers jurisdiction upon the United States district courts of the United States

C. Files
not noted

March 7, 1960

MEMORANDUM

Student Protest Movement in the South

Background

On February 1, 1960, four freshmen from North Carolina A & T College sat down at the lunch counter of a Woolworth store in Greensboro, North Carolina, and requested service. They remained for more than an hour, when the store closed: they had not been served.

What happened in Greensboro had occurred in recent years elsewhere in the South. The Greensboro incident grows in importance, however, because of the accumulating evidence that Negroes throughout the South saw in its example a means for release from discrimination and slights. These demonstrations have spread with such rapidity as to make crystal clear that the South is in a time of change, the terms of which cannot be dictated by one race. The deeper meaning of these demonstrations seems to show that segregation cannot be maintained in the South short of continuous coercion and the intolerable social order which would result.

Document 11a. Morrow's memo to Eisenhower regarding the student protest movement in the South, March 7, 1960 (Dwight D. Eisenhower Presidential Library). [National Archives]

The present wave of protest has had certain characteristic features which are likely to continue. For example, the movement has been spontaneous and contagious; it has been carried out by students; it has concentrated for the present on one sort of service -- lunch counters of stores which sell other commodities to Negroes: it has tendered to concentrate on branch stores of large chains: it has been generally nonviolent.

These "sit ins" mark a new trend in the Negro attack on segregation, adding to legal suits economic pressure and direct action.

The present wave of Negro protest may or may not peter out; it may or may not call for larger gain than a cup of coffee; it may or may not develop methods other than the present sit-in. Whatever turn events take, what has happened so far is a definite warning that the South must build into its societies social, economic and political practices which meet the needs and aspirations of the new order of Negroes.

Document 11b. Morrow's memo to Eisenhower regarding the student protest movement in the South, March 7, 1960 (Dwight D. Eisenhower Presidential Library). [National Archives]

Observations

It should be recognized that these Negro students have chosen a goal which no one can legitimately grudge and have pursued it by means which were selected after mature decision.

Negro adult leadership has widely and firmly supported the movement but has not directed it. Negro leadership feels that instead of expressing disapproval it has an obligation to support any peaceful movement which seeks to remove from the customs of the Southland any unfair practices based upon race or color.

It is also interesting to note that the Durham, North Carolina, Committee on Negro Affairs conducted a survey of the 5- and 10¢ stores located in Durham. The survey indicated that between 50- and 60% of persons entering the 10¢ stores were colored people. Obviously, therefore, the students' protest is against a system which accepts the business of Negro patrons while depriving them of the opportunity of the use of dining facilities.

Toward a Solution

Many responsible citizens are dismayed by events of the past week.
This includes not only persons who are dedicated enemies of Negro
equality but also those who are friendly to the Negro cause and who
have doubts as to the practical wisdom of the student protest. The
fact that these protests may lead toward violence gives pause to all.

There is sufficient evidence to conclude that one irritant which has
motivated the students is resentment over the pace of school desegregation. There is also much evidence to indicate that white
Southerners have almost always underestimated the extent of Negro
dissatisfaction. Consequently, they tend to be shocked when Negroes
demand something which Whites have hardly bothered to notice they
didn't have. In many instances White leadership in the South has
hardly yet begun to conceive the dimensions involved in these times
or to acknowledge that citizens must learn to live with these changes.

It would seem reasonable to state that the few stores against which
the protests have been directed should not have to alone bear the
burden of decision. This would appear to be a job for the entire
community of each city, guided and supported by elected officials
and civic leaders.

Document 11d. Morrow's memo to Eisenhower regarding the student protest movement in
the South, March 7, 1960 (Dwight D. Eisenhower Presidential Library). [National Archives]

The alternatives in the present situation are few and plain. One is to maintain segregation; this will invite a test of strength and will invariably lead to violence.

The second alternative is to eliminate the lunch counters completely. The third alternative is that of equal treatment. This is a decision that the business and civic leaders of the community must make and determine.

It is interesting to note that Oklahoma City was faced with a similar condition in 1958 and the Greater Oklahoma City Council of Churches took over and pulled the city out of its confusion, and in doing so has acquired the trust of both races. This solution might well be recommended to the beleaguered cities in the South.

E. Frederic Morrow

Document 11e. Morrow's memo to Eisenhower regarding the student protest movement in the South, March 7, 1960 (Dwight D. Eisenhower Presidential Library). [National Archives]

Resolution On Urging President Eisenhower To Visit The South

WHEREAS: In spite of the progress that has been made during the past year toward integration in the South, the fundamental fact is that the Negro people still remain oppressed and denied their basic rights, and

x OF 147-J

WHEREAS: Leaders of the Negro people have for many months now called in vain on President Eisenhower to visit the South, not for the purpose of playing golf at a vacation resort, but as a demonstration of the support of the President of the United States for the decision of the Supreme Court in the matter of integration in the schools and in public transportation facilities, and

WHEREAS: It was only by virtue of the fact that Rev. Martin Luther King travelled thousands of miles to Ghana in Africa and that Vice-President Richard Nixon, as a personal emissary of President Eisenhower, was confronted there with an invitation from Rev. King to visit the South, that the issue has been officially recognized by the White House, and

WHEREAS: Vice-President Nixon dodged Rev. King's invitation by urging him to come to Washington for a visit, now therefore be it

RESOLVED: That this Convention of District One, UPWA, AFL-CIO go on record calling upon President Eisenhower to give at least as much attention to our own country as has been shown to the problems of peoples in other lands in sending the Vice-President to personally investigate conditions, and be it further

RESOLVED: That we call upon President Eisenhower to make an official tour of the South for the purpose of investigating first-hand the denial of basic democratic and social rights to the millions of American Negroes living in that area, and be it finally

RESOLVED: That copies of this resolution be sent to President Eisenhower, Vice-President Nixon and Rev. Martin Luther King.

Submitted by
Local 347, UPWA, AFL-CIO

Passed by unanimous vote of
13th Annual Convention District Council #1 UPWA AFL CIO
April 5, 6, 7, 1957
Chicago Illinois

Document 12. Postal workers union resolution calling upon President Eisenhower to conduct a civil rights fact-finding tour of the South, April 6, 1957 (Dwight D. Eisenhower Presidential Library). [National Archives]

Document 13. Photograph, "President Eisenhower with Dr. Jonas Salk, inventor of the polio vaccine," April 22, 1955 (Dwight D. Eisenhower Presidential Library). © Wide World Photos, Inc. Used with permission. [National Archives]

Office Memorandum • UNITED STATES GOVERNMENT

TO   : The Director   DATE: March 2, 1960

FROM : Military Division

SUBJECT: Background in regard to your statement of February 28, 1960, comparing
the US and USSR space programs

There are two basic, but often confused, factors in making comparisons
between our program and the Russians: (1) space technology including weight
lifting capability and (2) space sciences. In effect, your statement took
the position that our lead in space sciences outweighs the publicly acknowledged lead that the Russians have in weight lifting capabilities. Usually
other administration spokesmen have discussed the two factors separately,
but at times they have been combined in general comparisons of relative US-
USSR position. Useful support for your remarks can be found in the following
unclassified statements.

1. Dr. Glennan, statement before House Committee on Science and Astro-
nautics, January 27, 1960. (pp. 3, 6-7)

"It is clear that the Soviet Union continues to hold a substantial space
lead in the eyes of the world. It is equally clear that this lead is
based principally upon the possession by the Soviets of one or more
reliable launch vehicle systems having perhaps twice the thrust of our
own first stage booster rockets.... In no other aspect of the space
business do we appear to lag the Soviet Union. In all other aspects,
it is my opinion that we have an equal capability and that we have
published more significant scientific results, more fully and more
promptly than they.... my statement coincides, I believe, with the
informed opinion of the scientific community at home and abroad....
But the fact remains that novel and spectacular space experiments
involving heavy and complicated payloads on difficult missions are the
big chips in this poker game at the present time....As individuals, we
do have a responsibility to recognize that while space is the most
glamorous, the most visible area of competition--and very fruitful also
for propaganda purposes--we are engaged in an across-the-board contest.
I remind you of this because these other areas of competition also
make large demands on the public treasury."

2. Dr. Kistiakowski, speech before the American Physical Society and
the American Association of Physics Teachers, January 29, 1960. (p. 3)

"Our scientific achievements in space have easily matched those of the
Soviet Union, notwithstanding the greater publicity given to the Soviet
technological spectaculars. This, I believe, is generally recognized
by the world's scientific community....So long as this /technological

Document 14a. Cadle's memo to the director of the Military Division
regarding the space race, March 2, 1960. [National Archives]

weightlifting/ superiority is temporary; so long as it does not permit
a vital military advantage; and so long as it is not across a broad
front, there is no need for alarm, but we must increase our efforts
to cancel out the imbalances that arise and are significant. On the
other hand, we must not permit ourselves to be stampeded into over-
emphasizing one area at the expense of others. We must constantly
bear in mind the sound military doctrine not to accept battle on the
field of the enemy's choosing. Rather, we must continue to move across
the entire broad front of scientific and technological advance. Thus,
as a nation, we will remain a world leader.

Document 14b. Cadle's memo to the director of the Military Division
regarding the space race, March 2, 1960. [National Archives]

3. Dr. Kistiakowski, remarks before the American Institute of Chemical Engineers, December 2, 1959, (Pages 1-2, 5)

"It is small wonder then that current Russian successes in rocket propulsion and some other technological skills, dazzling though they may be, are often described by the press as "scientific" superiority and thus given deeper significance than they deserve." "...USSR scientists, who also made important discoveries in outer space, cannot claim supremacy in outer space sciences." "...The Soviets excel at present only in a narrow sector of technology, as I have said -- the large sized rockets. But our own competitive instincts have been so aroused by their exploits in space that we feel an almost overwhelming urge to speed our technology in this field, so as to overtake or surpass them. If one separates civilian space science and technology from military missiles, which, as I noted, is entirely feasible, one wonders whether our insistence on superiority in space is of overriding importance. The unfortunate aspect is that space exploration has caught the public imagination to an extent that gives the Soviet achievements somewhat more importance than, perhaps, they rightfully deserve. The public reaction both here and abroad has been fostered assiduously -- and not unnaturally -- by the Soviet propaganda machine and, in a sense, by some of our own space enthusiasts. Viewed in the context of over-all competition for intellectual leadership in science and technology, however, -- and discounting the emotional and political factors involved -- our concern about space exploits might be questioned on grounds of reason and logic. It is characteristic of dictatorships that they are able to concentrate their national efforts more effectively than the democracies on limited objectives and thus gain a temporary superiority. Moreover, in view of the general strength of the USSR, it would be totally unrealistic of us to expect that at any given time we should be their superiors at every point on a broad scientific and technological front. We must accept as a fact of life that in certain areas, which will vary from time to time, the Soviets will be ahead of us temporarily."

4. Dr. Kistiakowski, remarks before the Delaware section of the American Chemical Society, October 21, 1959, (Page 7)

"As scientists and engineers, you should quickly be able to sort fact from fiction and to develop your own views on relative U.S. and USSR progress in outer space that you should communicate to your fellow Americans. To get you started, here are a few facts: At the present time the Soviets have an advantage in the weight of the payloads they are able to place in orbit or in outer space. This weight advantage stems from their earlier development of very large rocket boosters needed for their intercontinental ballistic missile program. Because of the United States' relatively advanced state of nuclear warhead development, we were able to develop an effective ICBM, utilizing a smaller rocket booster. There is thus no military advantage accruing to the USSR in the field of long-range ballistic missiles by virtue of her larger rocket engines, and the accuracy with which she is able to place payloads in space is certainly no better than minimal requirements for ICBM's. As regards outer space accomplishments, we must be careful to distinguish between pounds and payload. It is the design of the payload in terms of our scientific objectives that counts. Our program has already major accomplishments, as evidenced by the Van Allen radiation belts, solar hot spots and the Argus effects, achieved by highly sophisticated instrumentation in relatively small packages. This is not to say that we do not plan to increase our payloads and eventually undertake even manned exploration of space. But I would like to leave with you the thought that our space program will, in the last analysis, be no better than the quality of our observations and their interpretation. Our strong position in basic and applied research should keep us in the forefront in this new scientific arena."

5. Homer E. Newell, Jr., Assistant Director, Space Sciences, NASA, Hearing before the subcommittee of the House Committee on Appropriations, 1960 NASA supplemental appropriations (Page 48),

"Taking this approach one can say that the United States and the USSR appear to be at about the same stage of advancement in upper air research.···Likewise, the United States and the USSR seem to be at about the same stage of advancement in studies of the earth's environs where satellite techniques are adequate for making the necessary observations. In fact, it may be that in this regard the United States has the slight edge.···In deep space probe work the USSR has definitely taken the lead. This is directly attributable to their clear lead in vehicle technology.···A review of table 3 shows fairly clearly that the United States and the USSR scientists are at about equal stages of advancement in the problems they are attacking or are about to attack in space research."

cc: Dr. Reid

Document 14d. Cadle's memo to the director of the Military Division regarding the space race, March 2, 1960. [National Archives]

HOW COULD YOU KNOW
TONIGHT WAS THE NIGHT?

Everything was peaceful when you went to bed.

Not a hint of war on the late newscast.

How could you know they'd choose our town, tonight?

You couldn't. The enemy didn't want you to know.

    ★   ★   ★

But you could have been ready. Atomic bombs—and tornadoes, nres, floods—strike without warning. It's so important to be ready. So easy, too, now that U. S. Civil Defense has prepared a list of "must" first-aid items. Any drug counter can supply them. Every home should have them. Every family should learn how to use them.

BE SURE YOU HAVE THESE OFFICIAL DISASTER FIRST-AID ITEMS IN YOUR HOME

☐ 4 Triangular Bandages

☐ 12 Sterile Gauze Pads (3" x 3")

☐ 1 Gauze Bandage (2" x 10 yds.)

☐ 1 Gauze Bandage (1" x 10 yds.)

☐ 2 Large Emergency Dressings (7½" x 8")

☐ 100 Water-Purification Tablets (4 mg.)

☐ 3 oz. Antiseptic, Benzalkonium Chloride

☐ 1 oz. Aromatic Spirits of Ammonia

☐ 1 oz. Castor Oil Eye Drops

☐ 50 Sodium Chloride Tablets (10 gr.)

☐ 50 Sodium Bicarbonate Tablets (5 gr.)

☐ 12 Wooden Tongue Blades

Get free booklet "Emergency Action To Save Lives" from your drug counter or local Civil Defense Director.

SPONSOR'S NAME

CD-106   3 cols. x 166 lines (498 lines)

Document 15. Civil Defense poster "How Could You Know Tonight was the Night?"
1954 (Dwight D. Eisenhower Presidential Library). [National Archives]

SPACE BELOW RESERVED FOR COMMUNICATION CENTER

PRIORITY

5 Dec 57   17 21 z

PRECEDENCE		TYPE MSG (Check)			ACCOUNTING SYMBOL	ORIG. OR REFERS TO	CLASSIFICATION OF REFERENCE
ACTION	PRIORITY	BOOK	MULTI	SINGLE	AF	DI-18465	UNCL
INFO				X			

FROM: COMDR ATIC WPAFB/

SPECIAL INSTRUCTIONS

TO: COMDR, ADC, ENT AFB, COLORADO SPRINGS, COLORADO
ATTN: DIRECTOR OF INTELLIGENCE

RJEDDN.

/UNCL/FROM: AFCIN-4E4   12-1914-E

CITE UFO REPORT, DI-18465, DTD 27 NOVEMBER 57. RE USAF PILOT'S

SIGHTING WHILE FLYING F-86 AT 44,000 FT NEAR JOLIET, ILLINOIS.

REQUEST PRELIMINARY INVESTIGATION. OBJECT LARGE, FLAT, SILVER

COLORED, HAD GREAT SPEED AND PERFORMED ACUTE MANUEVERS. PILOT

REPORTS OBJECT CAME AT HIM AT HIGH SPEED AND THEN CHANGED COURSE.

CLAIMS HE OBSERVED OBJECT FOR 10 MINUTES. BELIEVE THIS IS

QUOTE UNIDENTIFIED AIRCRAFT UNQUOTE OF 100 SERIES, AND NOT UFO

REPORT. HOWEVER, AS REPORT IS OFFICIAL FROM USAF PILOT, AND

CONSIDERED IN A-1 CATEGORY, RESOLVING INCIDENT IS CONSIDERED

WARRANTED IN VIEW OF CURRENT RASH OF UFO SIGHTINGS. DISREGARD,

IF ACTION TAKEN.

COORDINATION:

AFCIN-4E4   [signature] DATE 3 Dec 57

AFCIN-4E   [signature] DATE _____

DATE 03	TIME 1115
MONTH DEC	YEAR 57

SYMBOL AFCIN-4E4 08 53	SIGNATURE [signature]
TYPED NAME AND TITLE (Signature required) Capt G.T. Gregory	TYPED (or stamped) NAME AND TITLE
PHONE 69216 PAGE NR. 1 NR. OF PAGES 1	ROBERT E. O'CONNOR Capt. USAF ...
SECURITY CLASSIFICATION UNCLASSIFIED	

DD FORM 173, 1 MAY 55   REPLACES DD FORM 173, 1 OCT 49, WHICH WILL BE USED UNTIL EXHAUSTED

Document 16a. U.S. Air Force report of a UFO sighting, December 3, 1957. [National Archives]

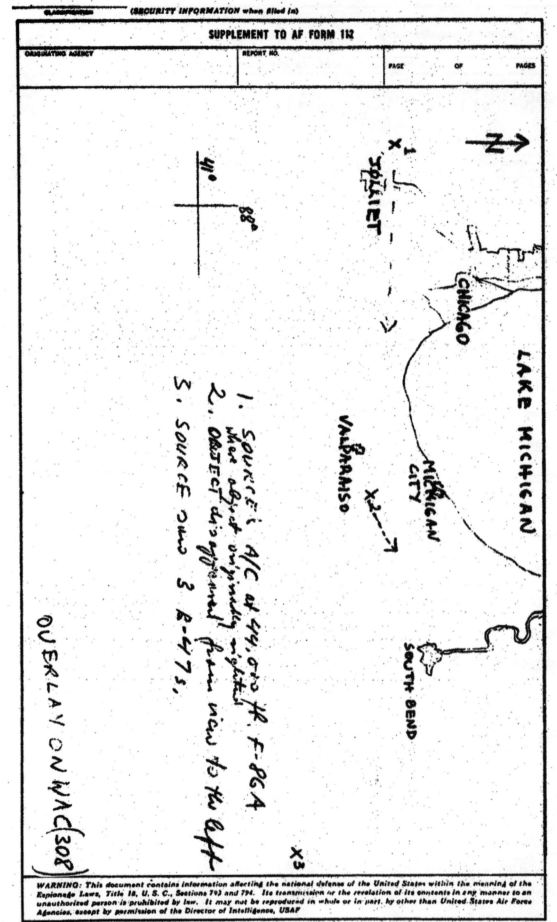

Document 16b. U.S. Air Force report of a UFO sighting, December 3, 1957. [National Archives]

Document 17. Photograph, "President Eisenhower with young pianist Van Cliburn,"
May 23, 1958 (Dwight D. Eisenhower Presidential Library). [National Archives]

39520
R-13/R-13
Russian

Dear Mr. President:

I thank you for your kind message of July 20, 1959, which was handed to me by Vice President Richard Nixon of the USA, who at the present time is our guest in connection with the opening of the United States Exhibition at Moscow.

We attach great significance to the reference contained in your message to the effect that the people of the United States of America and their Government desire to establish friendly relations among all governments, based on a lasting peace. It is the deepest and most sincere desire of the Soviet people and of the Soviet Government to bring about more quickly a definite turning point in the development of international relations away from the "cold war" situation and to bring about mutual trust in a lasting peace, in a broad development of political, economic, cultural, and other friendly ties among all countries and peoples.

Everyone realizes that decisive improvement in Soviet-American relations has and cannot fail to have a very important significance from the standpoint of strengthening peace and dispelling the anxiety of mankind concerning its future in connection with the threat of another war. Therefore, the Soviet Government welcomes

His Excellency
    Dwight D. Eisenhower,
        President of the
            United States of America

Document 18a. Translation of Khrushchev's letter to Eisenhower upon the visit of Vice President Nixon to the Soviet Union, August 1959 (Dwight D. Eisenhower Presidential Library). [National Archives]

the visit to the Soviet Union by Vice President Nixon,
with whom we had useful and friendly conversations
concerning the problems of strengthening peace throughout
the world and improving Soviet-American relations.

I avail myself of this occasion to express on behalf
of the Soviet people, the Government of the USSR, and
myself personally best wishes for the success and prosperity of the people of the United States of America in
all economic and cultural fields.

With sincere esteem,

/s/ N. Khrushchev

N. Khrushchev

The Kremlin, Moscow

August 1959

KHRUSHCHEV VISIT
Washington
September, 1959

59

S-E-C-R-E-T

KHV D-0/2

September 11, 1959

U. S. Objectives in Khrushchev Visit and
Suggested Tactics for Conversation with Him

I. Occasions for Talks

A. Initial call, afternoon of Khrushchev's arrival
(3:30 - 5:00 p.m.) September 15.

B. Weekend at Camp David, September 25 (6:00 p.m.) to
September 27 (12:00 noon).

C. At larger gatherings: President's dinner, September 15,
and Khrushchev's dinner, September 16.

II. U. S. Objectives

Our key purpose should be to impress on Khrushchev the urgent
need of a serious search for ways to reduce the dangers inherent in the present situation and of seeking an acceptable
basis for improved relations.

In pursuing this purpose we should try:

A. To make Khrushchev understand that, if the USSR continues
to act on its view that the balance of power is shifting
to the Soviet bloc and to attempt to enforce its will on
non-Communist countries (Berlin and Laos are current examples), the risks of war will increase as we intend to
honor our commitments. Arms limitation and control will
then become difficult if not impossible and the U.S. will
be forced to intensify its defense preparations.

B. To convince Khrushchev of our sincere interest in arms control but to make it unmistakably clear that adequate in-
spection and control is the minimum price at which it can
be achieved.

C. To point out the benefits to both sides of better relations but to emphasize that competition in peaceful
fields must be conducted according to accepted ground
rules applicable to both sides.

III. Probable

SECRET

DECLASSIFIED
Authority _STATE DEPT. LTR_
Date _6/10/76_
By _OJH_, NARS Date _6/28/76_

Document 19a. White House memo regarding U.S. objectives in Khrushchev's visit,
September 11, 1959 (Dwight D. Eisenhower Presidential Library). [National Archives]

III. Probable Khrushchev Line

Khrushchev will press for "peaceful co-existence." His recent speeches and his article in "Foreign Affairs" as well as the current Soviet line suggest that he will make or imply the following points:

A. The world must recognize that Soviet power guarantees the permanence of existing Communist regimes. "Peaceful competition" must proceed elsewhere.

B. Expanded trade is the best road to improved U.S.-Soviet relations.

C. U. S. bases abroad are the major impediment to agreement on arms control and to better bilateral relations.

D. "Re-militarization" of Germany is the major threat to peace and to progress on the German question.

E. A summit conference should be convened to discuss vital issues as decisions can only be reached on that level.

IV. Agenda

A. Khrushchev's initial call is scheduled for 3:30-5:00 p.m. The President might wish to cut it short and propose a helicopter tour of Washington.

The primary goal of this conversation would be to make Khrushchev receptive to serious talks at Camp David.

1. The conversation could open with some informal welcoming remarks and brief general conversation on Khrushchev's tour of the country. We tried to meet his desires and trust he finds the arrangements satisfactory. We would have preferred that it afford greater opportunity to meet broader and more varied sectors of our country and society. We hope he will come to understand the principles and convictions which motivate and guide our people as well as see how widely distributed are the benefits of our productive labors. Our papers, radio and TV are prepared to cover his trip thoroughly, but we hope

that

Document 19b. White House memo regarding U.S. objectives in Khrushchev's visit, September 11, 1959 (Dwight D. Eisenhower Presidential Library). [National Archives]

that this will not prevent his observing as much of the life of the country as possible.

2. To emphasize the urgency of serious discussion and implicitly the inadvisability of a propagandistic approach to the visit, the President might make these points - in a grave manner.

   a. Under present Sino-Soviet Bloc policy of pressure and crisis, the US and USSR seem headed for a sharp clash. The USSR could hardly have staged a more dangerous crisis than Berlin. As the President predicted in his July letter to Khrushchev, failure of the USSR to respond to the President's suggestion for a flexible Soviet position at Geneva has resulted in a distinctly less favorable atmosphere for the visit.

   b. The President and the American people cannot understand why the Bloc should have chosen this particular time to instigate another dangerous crisis, in Laos. (To emphasize this issue, the President might hit this point hard and often during the talks.)

   c. The US will not try to avoid a clash by backing away from its commitments. We have made our position on Berlin clear. We will fulfill our obligations to Laos.

   d. If Khrushchev seeks peace, he should use these visits for serious discussion of ways for ensuring that the competition between our two systems does not explode into nuclear devastation.

   e. If Khrushchev is disposed for serious talks on his return, he will find the President anxious to reciprocate. Such talks could lay the groundwork for fruitful subsequent negotiations.

   f. The President might conclude by stressing that he is not willing to submerge U.S.-Soviet differences in meaningless camaraderie. He and the American people are well aware of true Communist purposes regarding the United States

                                                    and

and other countries. He is in deadly earnest,
however, in seeking to find a basis for con-
fining the competition to peaceful fields.

3. Discuss and decide what will be said to the press.
We will probably want to keep it brief and general.

(Khrushchev may attempt to introduce substantive issues
such as Berlin and Germany or U.S.-Soviet trade relations. He is extremely forceful in conversations and
if we wish to avoid detailed discussion of substantive
issues, we must be prepared to deflect him. One way
would be to parry each sally by treating it as a suggestion of a subject for later conversations.)

B. Khrushchev will be at Camp David from the evening of
September 25 until noon September 27. This should afford
ample time for a full discussion of important issues.
However, in view of Khrushchev's tendency to long
harangues on subjects of interest to him, it would
probably be useful for the President to indicate at the
outset of each session what topics he intends to cover.

1. The central theme of the Camp David talks might be:
The major task of modern statesmanship is to find a
way to relieve the threat of destruction which
weapons of mass destruction have hung over mankind.
Khrushchev can make a great contribution to this
task and will be so judged in history, not by how
much power he can amass and wield. Continued Soviet
pressures will, of course, meet our determined resistance and the risk of war will remain and
probably increase.

2. Major topics for substantive discussions:

   a. Over-all U.S.-Soviet Relations.

   b. Berlin and Germany.

   c. Arms control, nuclear testing and the International Atomic Energy Agency.

   d. U.S.-Soviet bilateral relations.

   e. Laos.

   f. Communist

f. Communist China.

A suggested approach to each of these subjects is included in this paper.

3. It will be difficult, if not impossible, to avoid a joint communique. Khrushchev may propose unacceptable or undesirable wording that implies our acceptance of the permanence of Communist regimes in Eastern Europe, that hints at U.S.-Soviet "understanding" on issues affecting our allies, that leaves the impression that important divisive issues have been ignored or glossed over, or that suggests that the bilateral talks were a kind of summit meeting.

Document 20. Photograph of Moscow exhibit of the downed U-2 plane,
May 1960 (Dwight D. Eisenhower Presidential Library). [National Archives]

THE WHITE HOUSE

WASHINGTON

SPECIAL STAFF NOTE

May 19, 1960

From USIA:

<u>Summit.</u> -- On treatment of the breakup of the Summit
Conference, USIA has given its operating media the same
guidance provided to overseas posts directly from Paris
in coordination with the US Delegation. The tone is calm
and reasonable. Points made are that: the President went
to Paris prepared to consider in good faith the problems
scheduled for discussion; we are still ready to negotiate
on international problems and the present Soviet tactics
will not lessen our efforts; allied unity and US bipartisan
solidarity were once more demonstrated before the world;
we and our allies remain convinced that all outstanding
questions should be settled by peaceful means and not
through use or threat of force; Khrushchev was responsible
for torpedoing the conference (citing widespread foreign
comment to this effect); and the Soviet determination to
wreck the meeting was already fixed before Khrushchev
arrived in Paris.

Document 21. Special staff note on the breakup of the Paris summit, May 19,
1960 (Dwight D. Eisenhower Presidential Library). [National Archives]

REVISED DRAFT

STATEMENT BY THE PRESIDENT
UPON KOREAN ARMISTICE

July 26, 1953

We have all welcomed the news that an armistice has brought to an end the fighting between the armies of the United Nations and the Communist forces in Korea.

All of us share certain thoughts at this moment.

We think -- first of all -- of our brave sons who gave their lives to bring this armistice with honor. Their sacrifice has proved again the valor of free men.

We think of other sons wearied by months of imprisonment behind enemy lines. The swift return of all of them will bring joy to many homes. It will also be welcome evidence of the good faith of those with whom we have signed this armistice.

We think, too, of the enemy prisoners in our hands. We have steadfastly sustained their right to choose their own future, to live in freedom if they wish.

We think of our allies -- the soldiers and sailors and airmen of seventeen nations who have stood beside us throughout these long, battle-scarred months. It is proper that we salute particularly the valorous armies of the Republic of Korea, for they have done even more than prove their title to freedom. Inspired with the fighting spirit of President Syngman Rhee, they have given free peoples everywhere an example of courage and patriotism which again demonstrates that men of the East and men of the West, united in a just cause, can fight side by side in fraternal gallantry.

We are thankful to God that all of us have been able, through this bitter struggle, to give proof of the power of the conscience of the free world.   We have seen the United Nations meet the challenge of armed aggression -- not with words of pathetic protest, but with deeds of decisive purpose.

But one thought above all, at this moment, must discipline our emotions and steady our resolve.   It is this: we have won an armistice on a single battlefield -- not peace in the world.

This means that for the coming months, during the period of prisoner screening and exchange -- which we hope will be brief -- and during the possibly longer period of the political conference which looks toward the unification of Korea, we and our United Nations allies must stand guard against the possibility of untoward developments.

We shall take every precaution to see that the United Nations and American military position in Korea is not impaired during the armistice period.   For we know that manifest strength alone can guard the just and lasting peace we seek.

- 2 -

Document 22b. Revised draft of statement by President Eisenhower regarding the Korean armistice, July 26, 1953 (Dwight D. Eisenhower Presidential Library). [National Archives]

September 6, 1953, Denver, Colo.

Dear Mr. President -

Am writing you in regard to my son - 1st Lt. Barnard Cummings, Jr. 05942, P.O.W.

In the papers today, the news is that this is the end of the P.O.W. exchange.

Mr. President, may I write you as a mother, and tell you -- I know Barney is

being held and the evidence I have -- I want to make this brief.

My son, graduated from West Point class of '49.   He called on you with two

other classmates at your present address in the fall of '49.   You will recall him,

as he was the "remarkable" goat of the class of '49.

He went to Korea in August 1950 and he was one of three young men of his class,

who trained the 1st Ranger Co. in Korea (8th Army Ranger Co., 25 Recon.

Co. 25 Division).   These three men were made 1st Lt. right away, and had a long

period of very special training, and as I understand from his few letters, did the

kind of secret quiet work you do not write about.   This company was called into

battle on Nov. 25 1950 and were terribly defeated.   This particular company

was almost annihilated. The other two officers were saved, one seriously wounded,

the other man not hurt.   My son was reported missing as of that date Nov. 25, 1950.

×0 F3-R-3

These have been long hard years of waiting and hoping.   I've had the complete comfort

of God with me - my husband Col. Cummings, Air Res. died Feb. 14, 1953.

Now here is the evidence I have.   My son was alive in Jan. 1952,   An Associated

Press picture was released of unidentified G.I.'s receiving winter clothes, and Barney was right there in this picture. Everyone who knew my son is positive of this being him. It is not just my "wishful" wanting it to be my son. I have the press copy -serial number of picture -- I am trying very hard not to be an hysterical mother, but trying very hard to be the wife of a soldier and the mother of a soldier. I seem to feel very strong that they are holding my son particularly for his work with the Ranger Co.

Sen. Milikin and Sen. Johnson were personal friends of my husband amd myself who can verify who I am through both professional and personal in the years past.

Mr. President, thank you for listening to this. I know you do understand - for your very human kindness to all mankind. I feel you will open every door for me at this time when you understand this particular case.

Thank you - God bless you and Mrs. Eisenhower and all of your precious family - God bless you - and keep you well -for all of us in America.

Very sincerely,

Mrs. Barnard Cummings

857 Grant Street

Document 23b. Cummings' letter to Eisenhower about her son, Barnard Cummings, a prisoner of war, September 6, 1953 (Dwight D. Eisenhower Presidential Library). [National Archives]

MUTUAL DEFENSE TREATY

Between the UNITED STATES OF AMERICA
and the REPUBLIC OF KOREA

- Signed at Washington October 1, 1953

- Ratification advised by the Senate
  of the United States of America, with
  an understanding, January 26, 1954

- Ratified by the President of the
  United States of America, subject to
  the said understanding, February 5, 1954

- Ratified by the Republic of Korea
  January 29, 1954

- Ratifications exchanged at Washington
  November 17, 1954

- Proclaimed by the President of the
  United States of America December 1, 1954

- Entered into force November 17, 1954

Document 24a. Mutual Defense Treaty between the United States and Korea, October 1, 1953. [National Archives]

DEPARTMENT OF STATE

PUBLICATION 5720

[Literal print]

By the President of the United States of America

A PROCLAMATION

WHEREAS the Mutual Defense Treaty between the United States of America and the Republic of Korea was signed at Washington on October 1, 1953 by their respective Plenipotentiaries, the original of which Treaty in the English and Korean languages is word for word as follows:

(1)

For sale by the Superintendent of Documents, U.S. Government Printing Office
Washington 25, D.C.: Price 10 cents

Document 24b. Mutual Defense Treaty between the United States and Korea, October 1, 1953. [National Archives]

MUTUAL DEFENSE TREATY
BETWEEN
THE UNITED STATES OF AMERICA
AND
THE REPUBLIC OF KOREA

美合衆國 과 大韓民國 間의 相互防衛條約

Document 24c. Mutual Defense Treaty between the United States and Korea, October 1, 1953. [National Archives]

The Parties to this Treaty,

Reaffirming their desire to live in peace with all peoples and all governments, and desiring to strengthen the fabric of peace in the Pacific area,

Desiring to declare publicly and formally their common determination to defend themselves against external armed attack so that no potential aggressor could be under the illusion that either of them stands alone in the Pacific area,

Desiring further to strengthen their efforts for collective defense for the preservation of peace and security pending the development of a more comprehensive and effective system of regional security in the Pacific area,

Have agreed as follows:

ARTICLE I

The Parties undertake to settle any international disputes in which they may be involved by peaceful means in such a manner that international peace and security and justice are not endangered and to refrain in their international relations from the threat or use of force in any manner inconsistent with the Purposes of the United Nations, or obligations assumed by any Party toward the United Nations.

ARTICLE II

The Parties will consult together whenever, in the opinion of either of them, the political independence or security of either of the Parties is threatened by external armed attack. Separately and jointly, by self help and mutual aid, the Parties will maintain and develop appropriate means to deter armed attack and will take suitable measures in consultation and agreement to implement this Treaty and to further its purposes.

ARTICLE III

Each Party recognizes that an armed attack in the Pacific area on either of the Parties in territories now under their respective administrative

第 一 條

當事國은 關聯될 수도 있는 어떠한 國際的 紛爭이라도 國際平和와 安全과 正義를 危殆롭게 하지 아니하는 方法으로 平和的 手段에 依하여 解決하고 또는 國際關係에 있어서 各 當事國이 國際聯合의 目的이나 當事國이 國際聯合에 對하여 負擔한 義務에 背馳되는 어떠한 方法으로 武力으로써 威脅하거나 武力을 行使함을 삼갈 것을 約束한다.

第 二 條

當事國 中 어느 一國의 政治的 獨立 또는 安全이 外部로부터의 武力攻擊에 依하여 威脅을 받고 있다고 어느 當事國이든지 認定할 때에는 언제든지 當事國은 서로 協議한다. 當事國은 單獨的으로나 또는 共同으로 自助와 相互援助에 依하여 武力攻擊을 阻止하기 爲한 適當한 手段을 維持하며 發展시킬 것이며 이 條約을 履行하고 그 目的을 推進할 適當한 措置를 協議와 合意下에 取할 것이다.

第 三 條

各 當事國은 他 當事國의 行政管理下에 있는 領土와 또는 各 當事國이 他方의 行政管理下에 合法的으로 들어갔다고 認定하는

control, or hereafter recognized by one of the Parties as lawfully brought under the administrative control of the other, would be dangerous to its own peace and safety and declares that it would act to meet the common danger in accordance with its constitutional processes.

ARTICLE IV

The Republic of Korea grants, and the United States of America accepts, the right to dispose United States land, air and sea forces in and about the territory of the Republic of Korea as determined by mutual agreement.

ARTICLE V

This Treaty shall be ratified by the United States of America and the Republic of Korea in accordance with their respective constitutional processes and will come into force when instruments of ratification thereof have been exchanged by them at Washington.

ARTICLE VI

This Treaty shall remain in force indefinitely. Either Party may terminate it one year after notice has been given to the other Party.

IN WITNESS WHEREOF the undersigned Plenipotentiaries have signed this Treaty.

DONE in duplicate at Washington, in the English and Korean languages, this first day of October 1953.

FOR THE UNITED STATES OF AMERICA:

美合衆國을爲하여서 [1]

FOR THE REPUBLIC OF KOREA:

大韓民國을爲하여서 [2]

第 四 條

第 五 條

第 六 條

[1] JOHN FOSTER DULLES
[2] Y. T. PYUN

Document 24e. Mutual Defense Treaty between the United States and Korea, October 1, 1953. [National Archives]

Whereas the Senate of the United States of America by their resolution of January 26, 1954, two-thirds of the Senators present concurring therin, did advise and consent to the ratification of the said Treaty with the following understanding:

"It is the understanding of the United States that neither party is obligated, under Article III of the above Treaty, to come to the aid of the other except in case of an external armed attack against such party; nor shall anything in the present Treaty be construed as requiring the United States to give assistance to Korea except in the event of an armed attack against territory which has been recognized by the United States as lawfully brought under the administrative control of the Republic of Korea."

Whereas the text of the aforesaid understanding was communicated by the Government of the United States of America to the Government of the Republic of Korea by a note dated January 28, 1954 [1] and was acknowledged by the Government of the Republic of Korea by a note dated February 1, 1954; [1]

Whereas the said Treaty was duly ratified by the President of the United States of America on February 5, 1954, in pursuance of the aforesaid advice and consent of the Senate and subject to the aforesaid understanding, and was duly ratified also on the part of the Republic of Korea on January 29, 1954;

Whereas the respective instruments of ratification of the said Treaty were exchanged at Washington on November 17, 1954, and a protocol of exchange, in the English and Korean languages, was signed at that place and on that date by the respective Plenipotentiaries of the United States of America and the Republic of Korea, the said protocol of exchange recording the aforesaid understanding;

And whereas it is provided in Article V of the said Treaty that the Treaty will come into force when instruments of ratification thereof have been exchanged at Washington;

Now, therefore, be it known that I, Dwight D. Eisenhower, President of the United States of America, do hereby proclaim and make public the said Mutual Defense Treaty between the United States of America and the Republic of Korea to the end that the same and every article and clause thereof, subject to the understanding hereinbefore recited, shall be observed and fulfilled with good faith, on and after November 17, 1954, by the United States of America and by the citizens of the United States of America and all other persons subject to the jurisdiction thereof.

¹ Not printed.

In testimony whereof, I have hereunto set my hand and caused the Seal of the United States of America to be affixed.

Done at the city of Washington this first day of December in the year of our Lord one thousand nine hundred fifty-four and of the Independence of the United States of America the one hundred seventy-ninth.

DWIGHT D EISENHOWER

[SEAL]

By the President:
JOHN FOSTER DULLES
Secretary of State

U. S. GOVERNMENT PRINTING OFFICE:1955 O—57601

Document 24f. Mutual Defense Treaty between the United States and Korea, October 1, 1953. [National Archives]

TOP SECRET

MAY 13 1954

A CONCEPT FOR ACTION WITH REGARD TO INDOCHINA

THE PROBLEM

1. To find a way to resolve the numerous conflicting factors of the Indochina problem in a way which will preserve Indochina to the free world.

FACTS BEARING ON THE PROBLEM

2. The loss of Indochina to Communist control, either by negotiation at Geneva or by force of Vietminh arms, would have grave consequences to the free world.

3. The United States might be willing to intervene in Indochina if the following problems could be resolved:

   a. The U.S. must not be supporting "colonialism" in such intervention.

   b. The U.S. must intervene in some sort of allied action.

   c. The United Kingdom and the Asian nations related to her, particularly India, appear to be opposing U.S. intervention. This opposition is presently being manifested by "Asia for Asians" proposals based on the Colombo nations supervising and guaranteeing an Indochina settlement.

4. There are two further factors bearing on U.S. intervention:

   a. The need for Congressional agreement. This is at least partially contingent upon a clear resolution of the "colonialism" factor.

   b. The possibility of Red Chinese intervention. This is a somewhat separate issue presently allowed for in NSC 5405.

5. The U.S. is endeavoring to avoid the loss of Indochina and to resolve the colonialism problem by the creation of a regional grouping. It is not clear that a grouping adequate to resolve the colonialism problem could be used for intervention in Indochina.

DISCUSSION

6. To date there has been some lack of understanding amongst our Allies, "in Europe and Asia" as to firm U.S. intentions with regard to Indochina. This may arise because of a lack of an overall concept which will guide the U.S. as to its objectives and actions.

7. The following is an admittedly imperfect attempt to set forth a possible concept.

   a. The U.S. is unwilling to permit the loss of Indochina to Communist control by whatever means.

This document contains 2 pages.
Copy No. 41 of 41 copies. Series _____

I-12169

Document 25a. Memo, "A Concept for Action with Regard to Indochina," May 13, 1954. [National Archives]

b. The U.S. is prepared to join actively in two regional groupings. The first such grouping will include nations ready immediately to intervene in Indochina provided certain conditions are met. The second such grouping should be defined, with wider participation, to guarantee against Communist aggression or subversion, all of Southeast Asia with the exception of Indo-China so long as active fighting continues.

c. The smaller regional grouping, for active intervention, should consist of at least the U.S., France, the Associated States, Thailand and the Philippines. A precondition of its formation is the absolute declaration by France of the independence of the Associated States.

d. The second regional grouping should be open to all countries who wish to join, including the Colombo countries, Korea and, perhaps, the Chinese Nationalists. The Asian members, definitely including the Colombo countries, would be invited to maintain the peace and security of the area of Indochina progressively liberated according to the procedures set forth below.

e. Intervention in the Indochina conflict by the first regional grouping would be on invitation by the Associated States. Operations would be conducted from as many Vietnam held areas as possible to destroy organized Vietminh resistance therein and to develop a "front" which would delimit the areas of independent Vietnam. These areas would be expanded as rapidly as was consistent with the destruction of organized Vietminh forces therein. As soon as a substantial area was "liberated", the "active regional grouping, i.e., the U.S. and France, would turn over the maintenance of order, anti-guerrilla operations and anti-subversion to the Vietnam Government assisted by the Asian members of the second and "peaceful" regional grouping. Military installations necessary to support active combat could be kept as "enclaves" within the liberated area.

8. The above concept, complicated though it may be, would seem to resolve to a considerable degree the problem of U.S. intervention being construed as "colonialism." It would further be an offer to the Colombo nations to guarantee the progressive settlement of Indochina by force of arms in which they are not asked to participate. It would clarify to the world that the U.S. means what is has frequently said, that the U.S. is determined that Communist expansion by aggressive force of arms shall not be permitted.

9. The concept, to be effective in halting the deterioration of the free world position in Indochina and at Geneva, would need to be publicly presented to the world, after the decision to do so was reached by the Executive Branch and Congress. It would have to be presented in its entirety to obtain the psychological as well as factual resolution of the "colonial" problem.

RECOMMENDATION

10. It is recommended that this concept be given appropriate study and further definition by the interested Departments and Agencies.

2.

Document 25b. Memo, "A Concept for Action with Regard to Indochina," May 13, 1954. [National Archives]

République du Viêt-Nam

Présidence

Saigon, the 8th of November, 1960

Mr. President :

     The message that you have been so thoughtful to address to me, and through me, to the Vietnamese people on the occasion of the fifth anniversary of the Republic of Vietnam, has deeply touched me by the nobleness and the warmth of its feeling as well as by the comfort that it brings us, to the heart of each Vietnamese in Free Vietnam and, I am convinced, to that of our compatriots now living under the communist regime in North Vietnam.

     In the name of the Vietnamese people and of the Government of the Republic of Vietnam and in my own name, I extend my sincere thanks to you as well as to the people of the United States whose real and active friendship we appreciate at its true value.

     You have been so kind as to mention the numerous difficulties which the people of Vietnam have overcome, and the long way that they have traveled since the end of the struggle for independence, in the work for national reconstruction, and in the new fight that they must wage against aggressive and destructive Communism. Each success, each achievement, each sacrifice reminds us of the sacrifices which the great people of the United States have made so that the newly independent peoples could preserve their freedom, develop their resources, reach a higher standard of living.

. . .

His Excellency DWIGHT D. EISENHOWER

President of The United States of America

WASHINGTON D.C.

Document 26a. Diem's letter to Eisenhower on the fifth anniversary of the Republic of Vietnam, November 8, 1960 (Dwight D. Eisenhower Presidential Library). [National Archives]

The example that you have cited as one of the most significant achievements of free Vietnam illustrates in the most eloquent manner the work that we are determined to achieve here with the efficient assistance of the United States. Indeed the progress in free Vietnam is measured especially by the number of persons freed from misery and illiteracy, by the total area of rice fields allotted to tenant farmers, by the number of hospitals and classrooms opened to the population. American aid has proved to be a manifestation of the most striking form of international solidarity.

In spite of all obstacles, we are firmly determined to bring to a successful conclusion the present economic and social revolution which is based on justice and respect for the human being and directed to the benefit of the populace.

In this work as well as in the daily struggle which is at present imposed upon us by the actions of Communist imperialism, neither courage nor a spirit of sacrifice will be found wanting in the Vietnamese people, who have been accustomed to worse adversities in the course of their whole history.

Situated on the frontiers of the world power struggle, we look with confidence upon the strength of the United States as the shield for peoples threatened by Communist imperialism, because this strength is in the service of a just cause.

In conveying my best wishes for your health, for the success of the United States in the defense of the Free World, and in wishing for the American people an ever-growing prosperity, I am happy to renew, Mr. President, the expression of my most sincere gratitude for your message.

Document 26b. Diem's letter to Eisenhower on the fifth anniversary of the Republic of Vietnam, November 8, 1960 (Dwight D. Eisenhower Presidential Library). [National Archives]

MEMORANDUM

30 August 1954

From: 016
To: 00 = Adm Stump

Subj: Report on trip to Indochina

After leaving you in Saigon on 20 August, I proceeded with Rear Admiral Sabin to USS ESTES. The next morning the entire CINCPACFLT Pubinfo team (already in area) and I went ashore to Haiphong in order to travel to Saigon in company with Vietnamese refugees. We embarked in a French LSM which carried approximately 1,000 refugees to USS BAYFIELD (APA-33). The BAYFIELD transported a total of 2,000. We arrived Saigon 24 August. The following noon I departed Saigon for Pearl.

The refugees were almost all old, sick, or young babies. About 90% of them were Catholics and three of their own priests traveled with them. Until the time the Vietnamese reached the BAYFIELD, they received, what seemed to me, harsh treatment.

The herding of the refugees into the French LSM was rough. The deck was wet and people had to sit in the wetness. Many refugees had to sit on each other. Only half the ship was covered with awning. Everyone scrambled to crowd into the shady portions. Many were in poor physical shape. It was 104 degrees in the sun at Haiphong at 10 a.m. when the LSM got under way. Chief Photographer's Mate Cory reported that a Communist photographer was at the landing taking pictures of the "herding" operation. If it is true that the man was a Communist and his pictures are circulated up north, it will undo much of the propaganda which US Information Service is attempting.

The LSM took about five hours to reach the APA. During this hot mid-day period the refugees had no water, no food (except what they brought), and no head facilities. They were using the cloverleaf openings in the deck as heads.

The French are reluctant to let Americans help or give advice in any way ashore. Rear Admiral Sabin urgently needed to have a communications team ashore, but was denied permission by the French unless the team was integrated with their own Army. The day I departed, American medical officers had not yet been able to consult with the French regarding preventative medicine to refugees. The French were aloof.

I discussed this with a French officer at the refugee landing stage. He said, "You people have the job of supplying the money and the ships. Please don't try to tell us how to run our end of the show. We will run it the way we think best." I believe that this attitude is typical, although usually the French are not this candid.

After two days in the BAYFIELD the refugees (who had been in frightful condition at the start) began looking happy and reasonably clean. We asked did any of them want to make radio broadcasts to their friends up north to describe how the Americans were treating them. The refugees almost fought in their eagerness to get to the microphone. We made recordings and turned them over to the US Information Service in Saigon.

Document 27a. Memo from Lederer to Stump, reporting on refugees, August 30, 1954. [National Archives]

While the refugees were still in a happy mood we discussed with them (through an interpreter) the general conditions up north. As all of the Vietnamese gave approximately the same answers and as some of the answers conflict with what we have been told by the French, I believe their comments are worth noting. They are:

(1) A great number of soldiers fighting with the Vietmin are not Communists. But they hate the French more than they do the Communists. They are willing to take a chance with Ho Chi Min. No conditions, they believe, can be worse than present conditions.

(2) Whenever there has been political dissent under the French, the dissenter has been beaten, sometimes killed. Sometimes his entire village was punished by the French.

(3) The inhabitants of Vietnam (over the centuries) have learned that one must join the winning side to survive. Right now it appears to many of them as if the Communists will win.

(4) Vietnamese, in general, dislike the Chinese (who have attacked them for thousands of years). They would prefer to have nothing to do with them.

(5) At the time of Dien Bien Phu the Vietmin had only 60% as many troops as the French, and far less equipment. The morale of the Vietmin was so low that the officers had to do drastic things to get enlisted men to advance. If French had made an energetic showing all over Indochina at that time the Vietmin would have collapsed militarily.

(6) The French retreated over large areas without informing the loyal Vietnamese, thus exposing the Vietnamese to reprisals.

(7) Strong young people (at whom Communists are aiming) will not go south unless they have some assurances that South Vietnam will not go Communist; also that they have assurance of good treatment in South Vietnam.

(8) When the BAYFIELD neared Saigon, some of the Vietnamese expressed hope that the entire relocation would be in American hands; and some were under the impression that America was guaranteeing their happy future.

There are three important trends noted here: (1) American leadership and co-ordination in Saigon is weak at top level. (2) The French block most activities of Americans in Indochina and do not like to take our advice. We are spending approximately a million dollars a day in Indochina and yet have almost no control over political, social, or military events. (3) There is no sharply defined limit as to who is responsible for what. If the relocation of the refugees is a failure (and it well might be) the United States, and the U.S. Navy in particular, stands a good chance of being blamed by Southeast Asian public opinion.

RECOMMENDATIONS:

(1) The State Department should send a strong man to take charge in that area. He should be a man with an established reputation, one who can make decisions, and one who will not be led by the French.

2

Document 27b. Memo from Lederer to Stump, reporting on refugees, August 30, 1954. [National Archives]

(2) That American responsibilities in the refugee problem be clearly established and spread by every propaganda media throughout Asia.

(3) That a top propagandist with a team of experts go to Indochina to appraise the situation and start a professional campaign. This general topic will be the subject of another report.

Very respectfully,

W. J. LEDERER

TOP SECRET - LIMIT DISTRIBUTION

DEPARTMENT OF STATE
WASHINGTON

September 5, 1958

MEMORANDUM FOR MR. GORDON GRAY
THE WHITE HOUSE

SUBJECT: The Internal Political Situation
in Iran

The Under Secretary has asked that I reply to your
memorandum of August 29, 1958. The Secretary has read
this memorandum and approves of its contents.

We share Mr. Allen Dulles' concern over the situation in Iran. Most of the ingredients which contribute
to this concern have been with us for a long time. The
one new element involves the inspiration the Iraqi coup
may provide to certain elements within the Iranian military and others who believe that a forcible change of
government in Iran will resolve the many problems which
face the country. We are inclined to doubt that the
deeply rooted social problems of Iran can be resolved in
this fashion, and we continue to believe that the Shah of
Iran represents the best hope for evolutionary and peaceful change.

Whether the Shah will be successful in bringing about
needed reforms with sufficient speed to avert a coup or
attempted coup is a moot point. We believe, however, that
he has given us an opening through which we might be able
to help him gauge better the cross currents within his
country, and stimulate him to some constructive action.
We have authorized our Ambassador in Tehran to raise the
associated questions of growing dissatisfaction and desir-
able reforms at his next audience with the Shah. If the
Shah is amenable to this type of approach, some good may
come out of these efforts. There is, of course, no assurance that even if he is responsive to our suggestions,

this will

Mr. Lay has copy -
9-8-58

DECLASSIFIED

Authority *MR 83-541 #1*

By _____ *bc* NLE Date *2/3/84*

Document 28a. Memo from Smith to Gray regarding the internal political situation in Iran,
September 5, 1958 (Dwight D. Eisenhower Presidential Library). [National Archives]

this will enable him to ride out the rising tide of dis-
content. Indeed, the same could be said of any other
Iranian government called to grapple with inevitable economic, political, and social dislocations in an underdeveloped
country whose peoples have such new and unsatisfied wants.

Gerard C. Smith
State Representative
NSC Planning Board

Document 28b. Memo from Smith to Gray regarding the internal political situation in Iran,
September 5, 1958 (Dwight D. Eisenhower Presidential Library). [National Archives]

DEPARTMENT OF STATE
DIVISION OF LANGUAGE SERVICES

(TRANSLATION)

LS NO.   R-II

Spanish

Guatemala, Nov. 19, 1960

His Excellency
    Dwight D. Eisenhower
        President, United States of America
            Augusta, Ga.

I take pleasure in sending you the cordial greetings and the great gratitude of the people and government of Guatemala for the effective aid you were good enough to grant by ordering a watch on the seas adjacent to Central America by units of the glorious United States Navy, which prevented outside forces from giving support to the Communist-inspired revolutionary movement which, in connection with Fidel Castro, broke out in Guatemala on the thirteenth of the current month in order to overthrow the constitutional and anti-Communist Government over which I have the honor to preside.

This watch you ordered was decisive in stopping the development of the movement and greater bloodshed in my country and preventing eventual establishment of a new Communist government in the Americas.

The people of Guatemala, my Government, and I personally reiterate our friendship and gratitude to the great people of the United States, to its democratic government, and its illustrious President.

Miguel Ydigoras Fuentes
President of Guatemala

Fight Communism

with

"Truth Dollars"
for Radio Free Europe

Document 30. Advertisement for Radio Free Europe, 1954
(Dwight D. Eisenhower Presidential Library). [National Archives]

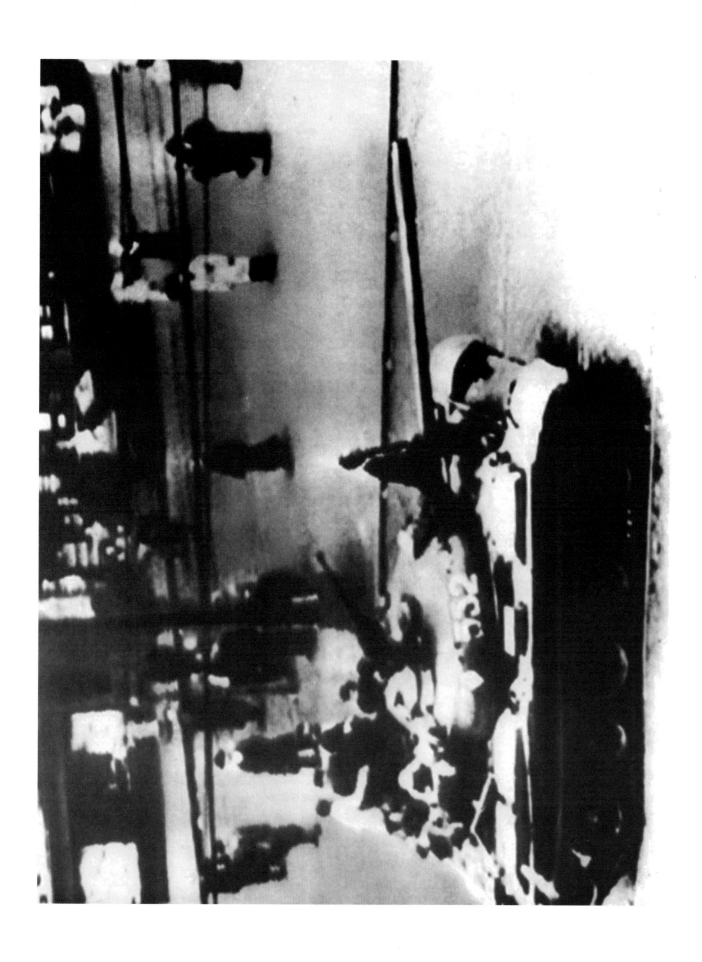

Document 31. Photograph, "Hungarian freedom fighters riding on a captured Soviet T-55 tank,
October 1956. © Wide World Photos. Used with permission. [National Archives]

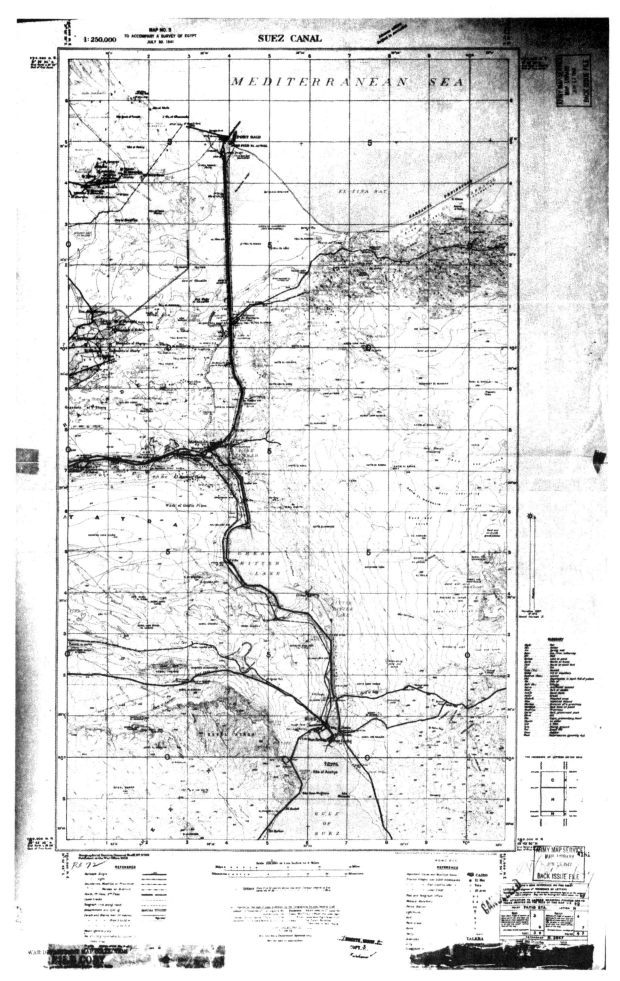

Document 32. Map of Suez Canal, July 30, 1941. [National Archives]

Document 33. Cartoon, "Images of the Fifties," January 1961 (Dwight D. Eisenhower Presidential Library). *Deseret News*. Used with permission. [National Archives]

The Gallup Poll

August 7, 1955   The Wash. Post

War and Peace in Ike's Favor

PRINCETON, N. J.—President Eisenhower's personal popularity—which stands today at a record high—reflects the public's confidence in a war hero who has now turned his efforts to working for peace.

On the one hand, Americans feel that a major factor contributing to his popularity is his brilliant military record. At the same time, they cite Mr. Eisenhower's attempts to bring about peace and keep us out of war as the thing that has impressed them most in his handling of the Presidency.

The chief criticism of the President is that he takes too much time off to go to the Gettysburg farm, play golf or fish.

These points of view come to light in an institute survey. Many persons cited personal traits as the thing that impressed them most about Mr. Eisenhower, with sincerity, honesty and fairness leading the list.

In answer to another question, many people feel that the Korean armistice, which occurred six months after the President took office, is the best thing he has accomplished to date.

The first question asked of a representative cross-section of American adults:

"How do you account for President Eisenhower's popularity with the people of this country?"

Ranked by order of mention, here are the top five reasons:

1. Military record.
2. Ability in handling job.
3. Keeping us out of war.
4. Personal sincerity and honesty.
5. His personality.

The second question:

"What one thing do you like best about the way Mr. Eisenhower is handling his job as President?"

The five top accomplishments, ranked by order of mention:

1. Keeping us out of war, peace efforts.
2. End of the Korean war.
3. Handling of foreign affairs.
4. Makes no hasty decisions.
5. Lets people know what he's doing.

The third question:

"What one thing do you like least about the way Mr. Eisenhower is handling his job as President?"

The five chief grounds on which the public criticizes Mr. Eisenhower:

1. Takes too much time off.
2. Favors big business.
3. Failure to reduce taxes.
4. Encourages segregation.
5. The farm program.

(Copyright, 1955, American Institute of Public Opinion)

Document 34. *Washington Post* article, The Gallup Poll, August 7, 1955 (Dwight D. Eisenhower Presidential Library). © The Gallup Poll. Used with permission. [National Archives]

Document 35. Photograph of President Eisenhower and congressional leaders,
March 6, 1959 (Dwight D. Eisenhower Presidential Library). [National Archives]

Document 36. Photograph, "Senator Margaret Chase Smith," n.d. [National Archives]

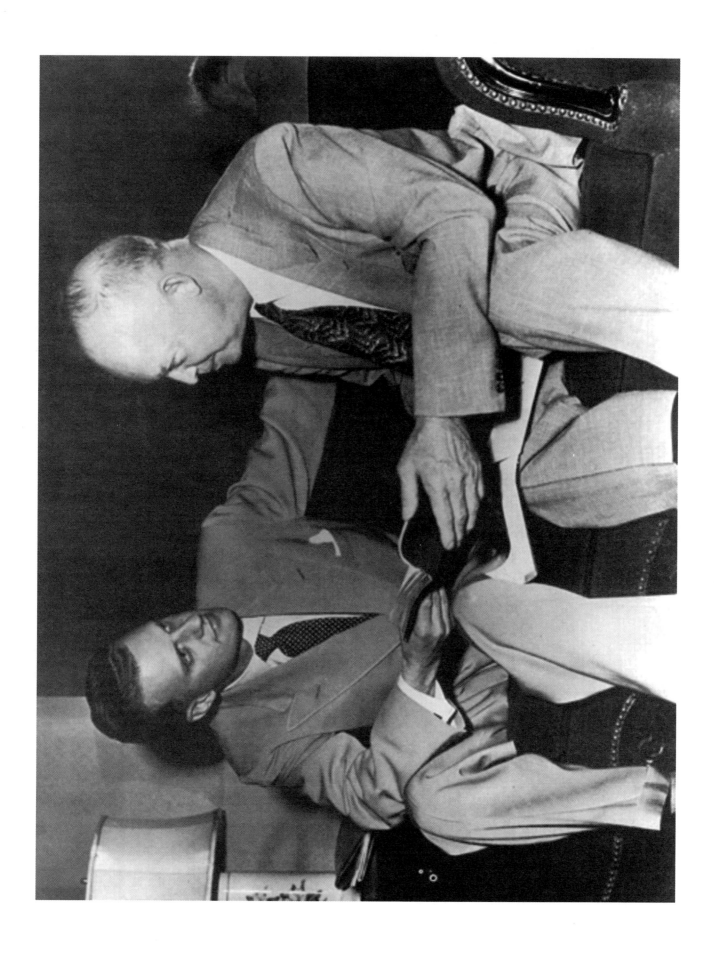

Document 37. Photograph, "Dwight D. Eisenhower with Billy Graham,"
August 8, 1952 (Dwight D. Eisenhower Presidential Library). [National Archives]

Box 755
Noxon, Mont

Dear President Eisenhower,

My girlfriends and I are writting all the way from Montana. We think its bad enough to send Elvis Presley in the Army, but if you cut his side burns off we will just die! You don't no how we fill about him. I really don't see why you have to send him in the Army at all, but we beg you please please don't give him a G.I. hair cut, oh please please don't! If you do we will just about die!

Presley
Presley
IS OUR CRY
P-R-E-S-L-E-Y

E R
lover

Elvis Presley
Lovers

Linda Kelly
Sherry Bare
Micki Mattson

Document 38. Fans' letter to Eisenhower regarding the induction of Elvis Presley into the Army, March 1958 (Dwight D. Eisenhower Presidential Library). [National Archives]

DEPARTMENT OF STATE
Division of Language Services

(Translation)

LS No. 51581-B

May 20, 1960 *

Dear Mr. President:

I was sincerely touched by the thoughts you expressed to me as you left France.

You may be assured that I share your feelings concerning the developments of these past few days. At least these developments have enabled our countries to test the strength of the bonds uniting them. That is a fact of which I was made very much aware during my recent trip to the United States and which is today more evident to me than ever.

I am certain that from this standpoint at least our meeting can have good results. Allow me also to tell you how much I appreciated the opportunity it has given me to find in you again the staunch friend you have always been.

Be assured, Mr. President, of my very cordial and faithful feelings.

Charles de Gaulle

*Note: Signed original is signed May 19, 1960.

Document 39. Translation of letter from French President de Gaulle to Eisenhower, May 20, 1960 (Dwight D. Eisenhower Presidential Library). [National Archives]

Document 40. Photograph of Khrushchev and Eisenhower at Camp David,
September 25, 1959 (Dwight D. Eisenhower Presidential Library). [National Archives]

Teaching With Documents Order Form

Peace and Prosperity: 1953-1961

You may order copies of the following document in its original size:

Document	Price	Qty.	Total
Document 32. *(17x22, b/w)* Map of Suez Canal, July 30, 1941.	$24.00		
Add 5% MD Sales Tax (if applicable)			
Shipping & Handling (Ground Shipping: $10.00, Air Shipping: $22.00)			
Total			

Billing Address:

_____

_____

_____

_____

Shipping Address: (if different from Billing Address)

_____

_____

_____

_____

☐ Check Enclosed payable to Graphic Visions Associates

☐ VISA   ☐ Mastercard   ☐ American Express

_____/_____/_____/_____/   _____/_____/   _____

Credit Card Number   Exp. Date   Authorized Signature

(_____)_____   (_____)_____

Telephone   Fax

Mail Order To: Graphic Visions
640 East Diamond Avenue, Ste. F
Gaithersburg, MD 20877